Praise for *Breakthrough Co*

Harrison Monarth, one of today's premier executive coaches, shows us how to use our own past successes to achieve new levels of meaningful achievement in his book *Breakthrough Communication*. Not since Dale Carnegie's *How to Win Friends and Influence People* has there been such a valuable road map for bringing high-impact results.

> Marshall Goldsmith, 2 million-selling author
> of the *New York Times* bestsellers *MOJO* and
> *What Got You Here Won't Get You There*

A practical and insightful translation of cutting-edge psychological science research.

> Laura Kray, PhD, Warren E. and Carol Spieker
> Professor of Leadership,
> University of California, Berkeley,
> Haas School of Business

If you want to be seen as the go-to person in your field, *Breakthrough Communication* is the book to take you there. Destined to become a classic, *Breakthrough Communication* tells the truth about achieving status in and dominating your niche. If you can handle the truth, this book will change your life.

> Kevin Hogan, PsyD, author of *The Science of Influence*

This book is a true breakthrough itself. If you want to learn to communicate better, you must read this book!

> Dave Kerpen, *New York Times* bestselling author of
> *Likeable Social Media* and *Likeable Leadership*

Breaking through to other people and getting results with communication is what inspirational leadership is all about. Harrison

Monarth shows how the process works in a thought-provoking series of steps that anyone can learn and practice. *Breakthrough Communication* is a smart and entertaining read for anyone who wants to be successful with people.

Debra Benton, President, Benton Management Resources, Inc., and author of *The CEO Difference: How to Climb, Crawl, and Leap Your Way to the Next Level of Your Career*

A compelling how-to for anyone who aspires to become a thought leader. The process begins with communication and some very essential skills.

Kitty Pilgrim, journalist, author of *The Stolen Chalice*

Monarth demonstrates his main points, right in his writing! Riveting information on how to get noticed, get your point across, and avoid strategic blunders. Great stories and well-researched, as usual.

Shelle Rose Charvet, author of the international bestseller *Words That Change Minds*

My concern regarding books on communication and persuasion is that they have always been short on what they promise: informing the reader how exactly to communicate persuasively. Harrison Monarth's readable (another missing component of most such works) book does precisely that and is an—perhaps *the*—invaluable treatise on the art of successful influencing in the business environment and beyond to get specific, identifiable results.

Richard E. Vatz, PhD, Towson Distinguished Professor; author, *The Only Authentic Book of Persuasion*; psychology editor, *USA Today*; editor, *Current Psychology*; professor, ILPD; University Senate; Towson University

BREAKTHROUGH COMMUNICATION

BREAKTHROUGH COMMUNICATION

A POWERFUL 4-STEP PROCESS FOR OVERCOMING RESISTANCE AND GETTING RESULTS

HARRISON MONARTH

New York   Chicago   San Francisco
Athens   London   Madrid   Mexico City
Milan   New Delhi   Singapore   Sydney   Toronto

1 2 3 4 5 6 7 8 9 0   QFR/QFR   1 9 8 7 6 5 4 3

ISBN   978-0-07-182880-2
MHID   0-07-182880-X

e-ISBN 978-0-07-183007-2
e-MHID   0-07-183007-3

Library of Congress Cataloging-in-Publication Data
Monarth, Harrison.
  Breakthrough communication: a powerful 4-step process for overcoming resistance and getting results / Harrison Monarth.
     pages cm
  ISBN 978-0-07-182880-2 (pbk.) — ISBN 0-07-182880-X
  1. Business communication. 2. Leadership. 3. Public speaking. I. Title.
  HF5718.M6456 2013
  658.4'5—dc23
                                                              2013032419

McGraw-Hill Education books are available at special quantity discounts to use as premiums and sales promotions or for use in corporate training programs. To contact a representative, please visit the Contact Us pages at www.mhprofessional.com.

To my darling Mom,
Roswitha Krems

CONTENTS

Step Four

ACKNOWLEDGMENTS

I want to thank my agent, Rita Rosenkranz, for her thoughtful support in finding the right home for this manuscript, and my longtime editor, Donya Dickerson of McGraw-Hill, for her enthusiastic attitude in embracing it. My thanks also to Professor Richard E. Vatz, whose work in the field of rhetoric and persuasive communication was the inspiration for this book; and to Andrew Erdman, PhD, Lydia Dishman, and Terri Peterson, PhD, thanks for their invaluable input in the early stages of the manuscript. I owe gratitude to my many clients who've enriched my life with their trust and the experiences that are woven into this work. Thanks also to my wife, who graciously offered her critiques. They were spot-on and made the end product better. And to my friends and family, thank you for listening and providing the comic relief.

Two Different Ways, Two Different Outcomes

A young child soon learns that life has its disappointments. We do not always get what we want, others do not always behave as we would like them to, and outcomes are sometimes—perhaps often—different from, or even at times the opposite of, what we desire. Many wise spiritual teachers, from the Buddha thousands of years ago through the present day, have gently, if persistently, reminded us of this truth. We can choose to reject it, or we can try to get comfortable with it.

Sometimes, however, things do go our way. The purchasing manager we have made our presentation to goes ahead and makes a big order of our product. The colleague we've been trying to persuade to collaborate on an important project says yes when we ask her for her support. The undecided voter who seemed disinclined to throw his support our way comes out and says, "You've got my vote." We feel good. All is right with the world. See, things do work out sometimes.

What is the difference between these two scenarios? Why in some cases do our interactions involving other people seem to turn out as we had wished, while in other instances we get "a rock," as a sad Charlie Brown so often realized? Surely it is worth recognizing that we can't always control outcomes. But it is also very valuable to know what we have done in those cases where things went right versus those scenarios where, for some reason, we ended up disappointed and befuddled. In fact, a thoughtful analysis of these situations can reveal to us that *we did do different things* in each case, that of the yes versus that of the no. In the former case, our actions and words have led to a *breakthrough*, a desired end. In the latter, quite often, we have left something out or have erred. What is the difference?

That is precisely what *Breakthrough Communication: A Powerful 4-Step Process for Overcoming Resistance and Getting Results* is about.

Breakthrough Communication presents clear, understandable, and time-tested concepts to help you maximize the chances of success after a communication process has taken place. That process may be seen in an instant—say, establishing a high-potential contact at a networking event or asking a busy colleague for help on a project. Or it may develop over the course of months or years, as is often the case in product development, policy implementation, or the improvement of an important interpersonal business relationship. The point is, there is a way to look at what might seem to be a bewildering, befuddling chain of exchanges as, instead, an analyzable series of events that can be handled more or less skillfully. Breakthrough communication, as I lay it out in this book, has four steps, allowing you to dive down into each successive component of your words and actions and make adjustments or, at the very least, examine in hindsight where you might have strayed from a more helpful and effective path. Furthermore, because of the coherence and clarity of each step, the tools used in achieving breakthrough communication may be generalized across situations. I recognize that my readers may be primarily engaged in business and enterprise. However, there is no reason why students, political professionals (and volunteers), and all of us ambling about and trying to make our way in the social world of our day-to-day reality cannot also make full and profitable use of this book.

Why Bother Communicating Better?

Why have I taken the time and effort to devise, revise, and perfect (to the best of my ability) these steps? My point is not to "improve communication" or to help you do something that our culture, media, and social rhetoric all seem to insist is important—communicate!—for its own sake. My true desire is to help you get results, to help you with the process so that you will arrive at the outcome you want.

Sometimes communication is described as an ad hoc process whereby two or more people reveal the contents of their thoughts to one another. However, I believe that this view of communication is naive, disempowering, and ultimately useless to the communicator who wants to *break through*—that is, suture the chain together so that another person or group of people become willing, in and of themselves, to listen. And act.

This latter view is crucial. In many settings, we all want to feel heard, to feel valued, seen, and recognized, to feel that our unique ideas and individuality matter. But in the world of business, politics, healthcare, education, the arts, and just about every other field of human endeavor, we also want our communications to result in actions. In *results*. Especially as leaders, the more responsibility we're given, the more we need to accomplish our goals through the actions of others. Simply getting the feeling that one has been listened to is not enough. We want to see that another individual has been so influenced by what we say or convey that he or she acts in a way that is consonant with our objectives: hiring us for a job, buying our product, exerting extra effort on a team project, saying yes to a proposed partnership, etc. Therefore, a communication situation has to have a measureable outcome. It either worked, in dollars and cents or favorable new behaviors, or it didn't.

Via enlightening examples from accomplished breakthrough communicators such as former secretary of state Madeleine Albright, Harry Houdini, Steve Jobs, Bill Clinton, Abraham Lincoln, Napoleon Bonaparte, Christopher Hitchens, and William Shakespeare, among many others, you'll learn valuable lessons of what to do and what not to do in your quest for breakthrough with others.

And while humans are freethinking individuals who cannot always or simply be persuaded to behave in a certain way (especially when it comes to spending their money or time!), the ideas and strategies in *Breakthrough Communication* will help you to more quickly identify situations in which it may be impossible to achieve a desired outcome, therefore alerting you to use your energies more fruitfully elsewhere or to quickly and appropriately alter a given objective.

Step One

CHAPTER 1

The Art of Getting on the Radar

What if there were a way you could learn to be lucky?

Think about it. How many times have you witnessed a positive event—such as when an old friend from college lands a plum job at a hot start-up, an otherwise quiet colleague serves up a winning idea that's implemented companywide, or your neighbor in the cubicle farm snags a coveted invitation to a star-studded industry party—and you chalked it up to luck? If any one of those people told you these opportunities landed in their lap after taking an advanced course in cultivating windfalls, you'd be signing up the next day—or perhaps even within minutes, depending on how satisfied you are with your current situation.

Now I'm going to let you in on a secret: you can start the course right away. To master the first lesson, every time you hear the word *luck*, swap it out for the word *opportunity*. As the two become interchangeable in your mind, it would make good sense to remember that opportunities (like luck) don't materialize from the ether. No matter if they're large or small, you have a choice whether or not to take advantage of the opportunities that can advance your career or help you leapfrog over obstacles. As we'll learn, opportunities are attached to people, so one way to capitalize on said

3

opportunities is to first identify the people or groups who can most benefit you and then look for ways to get on their radar.

A quick definition of what I mean by "radar" is needed here, though it's easy to get the idea. Being on someone's radar simply means that you somehow made an impact, however small, that can give you the chance to leverage the person's awareness of you for a deeper, more meaningful connection. And while none of us walks around with a gracefully arched, silver-colored radar dish strapped to our head, we all carry out unconscious sweeps to detect significant others in our social and work circles. The key word here is *significant*. The barista handing us our mochachino on the way to the office in the morning may get a smile and a friendly nod from us on our way in or out of the coffee shop, but he's not really on our radar. Most of us are hardly aware of a shift change at Starbucks and—casually indifferent—simply take our beverage from anyone who'll pass it over the counter. And we'll never give him a second thought.

Before people are open to hearing our suggestions, proposals, inquiries, or requests for help or support to a significant end, they need to consciously acknowledge the significance of our presence in their life experience. Before we get to present an agenda or issue to others, we need them to recognize us as important enough to listen to. This has less to do with luck and everything to do with harnessing opportunities to make an impression: on our boss (on whose radar we should be, but may also not be, if we blend into the background), a potential mentor, our colleagues, even potential new friends. If you can't get on the radar with key people, you might as well be invisible and—especially at work—miss a chance to land a high-stakes interview, get assigned a new client, get promoted (should have volunteered for that innovation project), earn recognition for a winning idea (that your more ambitious colleague decided to present because you felt uncomfortable), or make the most of any other opportunity that could propel you forward.

Speaking of missing opportunities, we all think we can spot them and make the right call in the moment, but reality is often different, and a narrow but definitive window of opportunity opens and closes in the blink of an eye.

I was reminded of this on a day I presented a workshop on executive presence and personal branding to 130 of AT&T's high-potential leaders from across the globe, at their company headquarters in downtown Dallas. My program was part of an extensive leadership development and networking program, and for that day, several top-level executives sat in the auditorium with all the high-potential managers, to take in my session. As I normally do, I asked for several of the present managers to introduce themselves and give a brief personal statement about who they were and what their value—not simply role or position, but actual value—was to the company. So if you were a sales leader, you wouldn't just say your name and identify yourself as a sales leader in a particular sector in a particular part of the country or world. You would mention how you generate revenue (make money) for the company by making sure that the people under you have all the support, training, and tools they need to once again top the previous quarter as "we've done for the fourth consecutive time over the past two years." Or something to that effect. Showing value is a powerful way to get on the radar with higher-ups. Guaranteed.

Since we had 130 people in the audience, I suggested that we have 10 people introduce themselves quickly at a clip of about a minute each, saving precious time for the actual program. What the managers didn't realize was that the introductions were a very important part of the program already and a lesson about to be learned. As I called for volunteers, sheepish glances to the left and right sought to unload my invitation on a neighboring seatmate. Slowly a few hands would rise ever so reluctantly as if to say, "Well, if no one else will, I guess I'll go. . . ." And so, like a dentist pulls teeth, I pulled a few volunteers out to give their introductions.

Mind you, these were "high potentials," meaning they were rising leaders in a company that has committed to developing their skills to become highly effective communicators and decision makers. They weren't frightened novices who'd never spoken up in front of a group of people before.

Seconds after the introductions, I flashed a motion graphic of a sweeping radar on a big screen in front of the assembled room. Then I said, "A moment ago, 130 of you had the chance to get on the radar with several high-level executives in this room. You had the chance to concisely and uninterruptedly share your value to decision makers whose interest you could have piqued, perhaps prompting an inquiry by them that might've led to an invitation to a personal conversation, face-to-face." And the members of the audience got the idea. A wasted opportunity to get on that radar, wasted for no good reason whatsoever.

So whose radar should you be on? Begin by thinking about the people who are on *your* radar and how they got there. Who stood out in a positive way, and why? Then make a list of the specific people who can help you achieve your own personal and professional goals. I'll give a few random examples you can tailor to your situation. For example, if you're an aspiring author looking to get your book proposal reviewed, you will need to identify which literary agents or acquisitions editors at a publisher would be most interested in your subject matter, based on their past choices. If it's a different position you're after at your place of work, your HR department may be a logical next step but not necessarily the most influential. There is likely a stakeholder or decision maker associated with that position who should learn about your skills, experience, and enthusiasm for the job. If it's a dream client you've been trying to get, you might think about who's currently on the potential client's radar who could provide an introduction for you or put in a good word about your services. If it seems daunting, consider this: right now, someone out there is trying to get on *your* radar.

Your e-mail box is likely full of those trying to get on your radar. You can help them reach a goal because you represent a link in their process. An unintended benefit is that by giving someone else a hand up, you can get on even more people's radar.

Opening the Door to Opportunity

It's not surprising that Reid Hoffman, a cofounder of the largest social network for business, LinkedIn, is a firm believer that opportunities are attached to individuals. In a recent article he wrote:

> If you're looking for an opportunity, you're really looking for people. If you're evaluating an opportunity, you're really evaluating people. If you're trying to marshal resources to go after an opportunity, you're really trying to enlist the support and involvement of other people. A company doesn't offer you a job, people do. Opportunities flow through congregations of people. Those with good ideas and information tend to hang out with one another. You will get ahead if you can tap the circles that dish the best opportunities. In fact, it's how people have gotten ahead for centuries.

As part of the executive team at PayPal before it was acquired by eBay, Hoffman says that though he and the others eventually moved on to different jobs, they continued to stay in touch and collaborate informally. When he started LinkedIn in 2003—something he calls one of the biggest opportunities of his career—Hoffman says he was able to get the business up and running at warp speed by simply tapping the intellect, resources, and investment capital of his corporate network.

With a current market cap of $19 billion, LinkedIn has earned a place in the firmament of legendary start-ups—handily beating

7

Facebook with an even more stellar IPO. But Hoffman is still busy connecting. He quotes author Steven Berlin Johnson, saying, "Chance favors the connected mind," and adds, "Connect your mind to as many networks as did Benjamin Franklin, Joseph Priestley, J. P. Morgan, and others, and you'll be one step closer to spotting and seizing those game-changing opportunities that great careers are made of."

In other words, don't hang back. Wallflowers don't get asked to dance, and reluctant networkers won't get on the radar that will open the door to opportunity. Hoffman recommends starting by joining smaller groups or connecting with local factions of larger national or international organizations. These can be alumni networks from your university, local business owners' forums, or special interest groups. Get in the door, introduce yourself, and start getting on the radar where it matters.

Putting Your Best Foot Forward

Just make sure that you're ready to get on the radar when it counts.

Two years ago, a team of psychologists from Canada, Belgium, and the United States found that there is some truth to the tired chestnut that goes, "You never get a second chance to make a first impression." Their findings, published in the *Journal of Experimental Psychology,* suggest that even though you might be a stellar human in all other regards, your tongue-tied attempt at small talk and your sweaty palms will likely take prominence in the mind of the CEO whose hand you shook at the last industry trade show, shortly after spilling that small plate in the buffet line.

"Imagine you have a new colleague at work and your impression of that person is not very favorable" explains lead author Bertram Gawronski, Canada Research Chair at the University of Western Ontario. "A few weeks later, you meet your colleague at a party and you realize he is actually a very nice guy. Although you know your first impression was wrong, your gut response to your new colleague will be influenced by your new experience only in contexts that are similar to the party. However, your first impression will still dominate in all other contexts."

Here's how to make sure it's a good one.

Nine Ways to Stand Out from the Pack

Obviously, getting on the radar in a positive light involves a bit more thought than making sure your shoes are shined and your shirt is clean, though both are important. It's a process that, if cultivated carefully, can open doors and windows to tremendous opportunity. And even though those first impressions can be peskily persistent, they don't have to remain set in stone. You can chip away at the negative ones with continued dedication toward presenting your best self in a variety of new contexts—and far away from the finger food.

Present like a Pro

No matter what industry you're in, presenting proposals, information, and ideas is likely part of your professional (and personal) existence. Better do it well then. Brilliant contributors who can't convince or persuade or at least engage long enough to get an important point across are quickly marginalized in favor of those who can. The statement "How you say something is more important than what you say" is false on its face, but it's well intended. Presenting with passion and conviction while engaging an audience's emotions is important, but so is having a concise, meaningful, and relevant message—structured with chosen words for impact—that plants just the right seeds in the minds of an audience. Learning how to do this well requires study and practice. Shun tired clichés, bland visuals, overloaded PowerPoint slides, and rambling data dumps that the audience can't possibly process without mentally fatiguing minutes after the information onslaught begins. Instead, present briefly, in as simple a wording as possible, with slides lean and mean, relevant and clear points with just enough detail to get the message across. And act like your life depends on the people in the audience "getting it." Then they know you really care, and they might deem it important enough to care as much.

Cultivate a Reputation of Expertise

Before you clutch your heart in terror that you'll need a PhD, several published books, and an appearance on *The Colbert Report* to be acknowledged as an expert, take a deep breath. Now understand that there is an important difference between having expertise and being an expert. The latter requires all the trappings of a life's work, homing in on a particular subject and being able to expound on it with fluency and inspire the reverence of all who listen.

Fortunately, we don't need to be bona fide experts in order to get on the radar. In fact, the moniker is overrated. Economist Noreena Hertz contends that we, as a society, become less innovative and less likely to be able to make our own decisions when we are being spoon-fed by experts. Not to mention that so-called experts can make mistakes, too. Hertz notes that doctors misdiagnose 4 times out of 10 and that we are statistically more likely to file our tax returns correctly than a tax advisor.

Instead of striving for hallowed expert status, spend a moment thinking about the experiences you have cultivated and all the good work you've already done. For those just starting out or embarking on a different career, make a list of all the skills you've already acquired such as time or project management, leadership in any team or group, the ability to self-direct, attention to detail, superior writing skills, etc. These are all qualities that can add up to important slivers of expertise in a particular field and ingredients that can distinguish you to help get you on the radar.

Embrace Leadership via Skill and Dominance

The next time you are in a roomful of people, take note of who draws the most eyeballs. You may be surprised to find that it's not always Miss Congeniality or the affable guy from accounting who seems to know everyone's name. A new study from the University of British Columbia published in the *Journal of Personality and Social Psychology* found that two sets of behaviors catch people's attention: prestige, via the appearance of skill and competency, and dominance.

"Our findings suggest there are really two ways to top the social ladder and gain leadership—impressing people with your skills or powering your way through old-fashioned dominance," says lead author Joey Cheng, a PhD candidate in UBC's Department of Psychology. "By measuring levels of influence and visual attention, we find that people defer to and readily spot the prestigious and dominant leaders."

Likability has long been cited as an important influence strategy, and yet by asserting yourself in group dynamics by standing up for what you believe in and by making your voice and opinion heard, you can attract that critical attention that lands you on others' radar. Equally important a strategy to get on the radar and influence opportunities, you need to be able to exude an air of competence. How to do this without impeccable and long-earned credentials? You can assert your credibility by being able to speak knowledge-ably—perhaps by sharing expertise—to the people whose radar you are trying to tip your way, making them feel certain you, or your product or service, can meet their particular needs.

Write E-mails People Can't Ignore

Sometimes the only way to get on someone's radar is through e-mail. If you are like most people, you're rolling your eyes at the probability (or lack thereof) that your target will be wading through a clogged inbox and instantly single out your message.

Think positive. In the war against an endless tide of electronic mail, you have the strategic weapons to get your message seen and get on the recipient's radar. Crafting messages with a clear objective and concise and unambiguous wording can distinguish your e-mail in a welcomed way. In a piece for the *Harvard Business Review*, Bryan Garner offers a plan of attack, starting with composing a pithy and actionable subject line. Those left vague (e.g., "checking in," "follow up")—or worse, left blank—inspire nothing more than a pass or delete.

Setting up the request (for a meeting or invitation) in the subject line should be followed by getting right to the point in your note. Be polite, organize your thoughts in a coherent way, and keep it brief. This is not the place to expound on your expertise. Simply make your request and suggest a firm deadline for the person to get back to you.

Expect to Be Accepted

Another key component of getting on the radar is to be optimistic about your chances. Don't let the jitters of making an impression on a busy executive or a strategically placed industry professional get the better of you, especially if you are meeting the person for the first time.

We didn't need the paper published in *Personality and Social Psychology Bulletin* to suggest that the interpersonal warmth that people project predicts how much others like them; this is, by now, surely common sense. Notable though is the finding that people who consciously expected to be accepted did act more warmly toward a stranger and consequently they were perceived as more likable.

Though the study is controversial, it can never hurt to be a "social optimist." Having a positive outlook that you'll be able to get on the radar of the people you've singled out can only add to the confidence you'll exude after preparing to meet them by taking stock of your expertise and building up an air of competence.

Make the Most of Your Looks

It never hurts to look your best.

Professor V. Bhaskar, from University College London, who participated in a 2008 study published in *New Scientist* magazine, found that although looks had no bearing on the study group's performance on a game show, less attractive people were twice as likely to be booted off as their better-looking, yet no better-performing, competitors. Physical appearance was the deciding factor, the researchers found, as contestants ignored other features such as age or sex.

If you haven't been blessed with the kind of looks that would earn you a starring role in a big-budget Hollywood film, don't fret. Work with what you have to put your best face forward. For both men and women this means having a hairstyle that flatters one's face and is up-to-date, decadewise. It means checking your teeth for unsightly stains, chips, or other dental distractions and making a visit to the dentist. To achieve a well-rested, vibrant glow, a combination of good nutrition, plenty of water, regular exercise, and the occasional facial at the capable hands of a Ukrainian aesthetician can make the difference between a thumbs-up or thumbs-down from those with whom we interact.

Get Bonus Points for Flirting?

Batting eyelashes or laying on a thick layer of charm works every time in the average Hollywood flick, but will it help you get on the radar in personal and work circles? A study entitled "Feminine Charm: An Experimental Analysis of Its Costs and Benefits in Negotiations" suggests that it does, but mostly for women and only when it isn't sexual.

Haas School of Business professor Laura Kray found that authentic, engaging behavior without serious intent signals attractive qualities such as confidence—a key ingredient of successful negotiators. And it's not just for those merely aspiring to the top jobs. Former U.S. secretary of state Madeleine Albright reportedly responded in the affirmative when asked by comedian Bill Maher whether she ever flirted with the predominantly male heads of state she met in negotiations. Kray found that women who said they used more social charm were rated more effective by their business associates and partners. Men wielding the same, however, not so much.

Embrace Personal Branding

Your personal brand—what others perceive of you—plays a big part in getting you on someone's radar. Your car, your clothes, your mood and attitude at work, your handshake, your input and demeanor in meetings, the way you communicate (or don't), and the way you handle projects—they all add up to create the powerful mosaic that is your personal brand.

While most of us behave unconsciously in the tens of thousands of moments that make up a day, in order to create the maximum impact once you're on someone's radar, you need to adopt a controlled approach, a la *Mad Men's* Don Draper, to ensure your branding will be every bit as effective as the campaigns he dreamed up for the likes of Hilton and Jaguar.

Tom Peters revolutionized this concept back in 1997 when he wrote an article titled "The Brand Called You" for *Fast Company Magazine*. In it, he said, "The good news—and it is largely good news—is that everyone has a chance to stand out. Everyone has a chance to learn, improve, and build up their skills. Everyone has a chance to be a brand worthy of remark."

He argues that you can put yourself among the ranks of Coke, Nike, and other global brands by starting small and growing your power and influence, one interaction at a time. Peters wrote:

There are power trips that are worth taking—and that you can take without appearing to be a self-absorbed, self-aggrandizing megalomaniacal jerk. Is your team having a hard time organizing productive meetings? Volunteer to write the agenda for the next meeting. You're contributing to the team, and you get to decide what's on and off the agenda. When it's time to write a post-project report, does everyone on your team head for the door? Beg for the chance to write the report—because the hand that holds the pen (or taps the keyboard) gets to write or at least shape the organization's history.

Peters suggests that acting like a leader makes you a leader. Getting on the radar works the same way. As I've written in my previous book *Executive Presence*, this requires being keenly aware of everything you put out there, from your appearance to your social energy to the way you conduct yourself on the job and manage relationships. Match that awareness with an understanding of how you are perceived by others and how you are valued, and you are on your way to securing a spot on anyone's radar.

Recall that, at the beginning of this chapter, I recommended you start working toward your professional and personal goals by swapping luck for opportunity. It's never more necessary than when you are building your personal brand. Instead of relying on fate or the universe to buffet you around on life's journey, put yourself in the way of approaching opportunity. Your personal brand will become the message you consciously send to others and a primary element of the process of attracting that "good fortune."

Navigate Organizational Politics

The importance of this cannot be overstated and applies whether you've been part of an organization for years or you've just joined. A strong personal brand—which by the way should always be in development and never static—will aid breakthrough communicators as they actively work on navigating the interpersonal dynamics of the group they aim to influence; and this is really the crux of office politics. Personal branding and interpersonal politics go hand in hand as they define the waters of these subcultures, and your ability to swim relies on how you present yourself within them.

From the water cooler to a corner of the cubicle farm, from the outer reaches of a staff that works remotely from any country in the world to the hyperlocal group of independent business owners, you will be moving in circles that have their own dynamics and ways of getting things done. In order to get on anyone's radar within these networks, you'll have to learn how best to approach and how to operate effectively within the person's unique cultural environment.

The key here is awareness. Observe the group and how your targeted person or people are moving within it. Assess how they like to be approached by how they respond and from what others say about them. Learn as much as you can; then make an effort to engage. While an in-person introduction by an influential colleague or a recommendation by an esteemed so-and-so would top the list of ways to get on their radar, those aren't always available options. Be determined to reach out and introduce yourself anyway. Done with confidence and a healthy dose of social intelligence, you'll find most people respond favorably. A mix of confidence and appropriate humility is a killer combo when approaching virtual strangers.

If you are wavering, take stock of your own power within your current networks. Beyond the inherent power of your title and the size of your paycheck, observe closely how people react when you ask them to do something for you or how often you're approached for advice and assistance. The answers will hint at where you stand and what work lies ahead for you, if you are willing to engage.

Jeffrey Pfeiffer, who teaches business at Stanford University, contends that competence is not enough to catapult people into the orbit of success, but they don't have to be gifted, either. What is necessary is that they're willing to take risks.

The Risk and Rewards of Using Social Media to Get on the Radar

At Columbia's Graduate School of Journalism, Sree Sreenivasan, dean of student affairs and a professor who has been teaching digital journalism, told the *New York Times* last year, "We have to think about social media in a new strategic way. It is no longer something that we can ignore. It is not a place to just wish your friends happy birthday. It is a place of business. It is a place where your career will be enhanced or degraded, depending on your use of these tools and services."

However virtual, social media has become a powerful and easy way to connect with people you would never have met in real life. Not only has this spurred a rise in the number of jobs on Mediabistro's job board in the categories of mobile, social media, web development, and social-app gaming by 140 percent since 2010, but it provides countless opportunities for people from any industry to get on the radar of their person or company of choice.

Take Havard Rugland, a 28-year-old from a small town in Norway. He didn't know the first thing about American football, but thanks to a homemade video of his kicking prowess that he posted on YouTube, he earned the chance to try out for the NFL.

Eye-popping kicking stunts notwithstanding (he punted one ball and then immediately kicked another, and the two collided midair), Rugland's skill with Facebook and Skype went a long way to getting him on the New York Jets coaches' radar.

Just keep in mind that social media is deceptively simple to use and therefore potentially risky. Asynchronous communication has a way of rendering even the most humorous of 140-character tweets seem stale and tactless the following day. And Facebook photos of you partying hard (even though they are from your college days) are not likely to impress a prospective boss or new client.

If you are planning to use social media channels to get on people's radar, start as you would in real life. Join a LinkedIn group they are a member of, post an interesting discussion topic, or follow and participate in a hashtagged discussion on Twitter.

To approach more directly, remember that if they are as busy as you think they are, the last thing they'll have the proverbial bandwidth for is lavishing their attention on a stranger who wants to pick their brain—even if that stranger is offering to buy the lattes.

Instead respect their limited availability and approach them with a laser-focused question along with that LinkedIn request to connect. Nothing turns a busy person's radar sensor off more quickly than a vague invitation to "join their professional circle" or an open-ended appeal for mentorship. The social media connections most likely to get a useful reply are those that pose a concrete request or offer a value that truly resonates, which means you have to know a little more about the person than just his or her job title and employer. It's up to you to zero in on what you really want from the person and then deliver your targeted inquiry or tailored offer in the social channel of choice.

In the next chapter we'll talk about the importance of status and how a strategic blend of high-, medium-, and low-status communication can yield the biggest benefits for getting on people's radar.

CHAPTER 2

Managing Your Status

This chapter won't ask you define yourself using concepts put forth by Plato and Aristotle, where everything on earth is bounded by a hierarchical structure starting with God and progressing downward through the ranks of angels and demons, royalty and regular folk, to animals, plants, and rocks. You already know what position we humans hold in that Great Chain of Being. Instead, I ask you to consider where you stand in relation to the decision maker(s) you seek to influence.

Considering Status: Where Do I Stand?

This is not a rhetorical question. The good news is, it's not a philosophical one, either. Consider these questions: Are you influential or famous? Or are you, more likely, a "mere civilian"? Who are the other parties? What is their status? Are you affiliated with some kind of larger group or institution that you can leverage to change the status picture?

By asking yourself these questions, you'll be taking the first step toward developing more self-awareness, a cornerstone in the greater concept of emotional intelligence. This isn't only a neat party trick to be deployed when you're meeting new people at a corporate function or policing the punch bowl at the annual holiday soiree. It's a way for you to adjust, monitor, and leverage your status to get and stay on anyone's radar.

The Difference Between Status and Power

Part of what makes or breaks an individual's position is the person's status and power. There is a big difference between the two, and that difference exists in the order of just about any social system—democratic or totalitarian. Knowing the difference can help you get on the radar to get ahead or even just get along.

NYU's Stern School of Business professor Steven Blader and Cornell University professor Ya-Ru Chen wrote an article titled "Differentiating Effects of Status and Power," published in the *Journal of Personality and Social Psychology*. In it, they define the important conceptual differences between status and power this way: "Status is the prestige, respect and esteem that a party has in the eyes of others . . . an index of the social worth that others ascribe to an individual or a group. Status originates externally and is rooted in the evaluations of others through status-conferral processes."

On the other hand, Chen and Blader believe, "Power is best conceptualized as control over critical resources—that is, outcome control." In other words, other people will grant an individual status depending on the person's behavior and achievements. Power is the ability to hold the reins, whether you've taken them by your own merit or grabbed them away from someone else.

The two contend that although power and status are often thought of as two sides of the same coin, "they in fact have opposite effects on the fairness of people's behavior." To prove it, Chen and Blader experimented with a variety of groups including one in which nearly 200 MBA students took part in a 25-minute negotiation exercise. Each person was assigned the role of a CFO of one of two pharmaceutical companies and was tasked with working out the terms of a deal.

Three subgroups were formed. One was given "status"; that is, the people in this subgroup were told they were some of the most respected people in the industry. The members of the "power" group were told their company was highly profitable and thanks to their connections they had access to plentiful resources. The third group wasn't given a specific condition. Can you guess who played most fairly? The researchers found that those with status treated others much more fairly, whereas members of the power group tended to be more dismissive.

Do you know where you stand on the power-versus-status meter?

Measuring Personal Power Versus Status

People are like dogs, researchers Sanjay Srivastava of the University of Oregon and Cameron Anderson of the University of California, Berkeley, suggested in a paper they published about perceiving power and status in social groups, titled "Accurate When It Counts: Perceiving Power and Status in Social Groups."

They contend that the key to interacting successfully with dogs, which are highly social and travel in packs, is to understand the two questions that the animal cares about: (1) Who is dominant? and (2) who likes me?

The authors present a case that most people, much of the time, are better at perceiving their own and others' power and status than they are at gauging their own likability or personality traits. Why are we better at the former? In part because of visible cues. People who are extroverted or physically attractive are more likely to attain status in groups, and individuals with dominant personalities can often be singled out from a postage-stamp-sized avatar

21

because they tend to have distinct facial features. Once in positions of power, people will often demonstrate more confidence in their body language as well as speak more confidently.

Wouldn't it be too easy, then, to think you have more power or status than you actually do? Srivastava and Anderson write, "We hypothesized that the theory of positive illusions does not apply to status. Because it is so important to know one's own status in a group context, and because overestimating one's own status carries particular costs, we hypothesized that self-perceptions of status would either be neutral or even slightly self-effacing."

That's not to say that the basic human motivation to belong isn't trumped by people who have an inflated sense of self-importance. Unless you are a complete narcissist, though, your perception of your own status and power is well within your grasp. Just make sure to use both wisely.

A widely used tool in the corporate world—it is said that approximately 90 percent of Fortune 500 firms use some form of it—is the 360-degree feedback survey, also known as multi-rater feedback. The "360" gathers anonymous feedback from the immediate environment of an employee—that person typically being a high-potential manager or executive on the rise—including peers, subordinates, and supervisors. Recipients of a 360 also take part in the process via self-evaluation, and the difference between one's self-perception and those of others can be highly informative and inspiring, or it can be quite humbling, depending on the spirit in which the information is received. Either way, the only way of learning of one's perceived status is by listening to what others think, as it is they who confer status in the first place.

For those who don't work for a Fortune 500 company or an organization that invests in its employees' development via a 360, there are other, more rudimentary ways of getting a more balanced picture of one's status and perceived leadership. The basics are the same; think about who has had ample opportunity to observe you in action. One caveat: since the raters wouldn't be anonymous, you'd have to make it clear that they have full permission to be brutally honest; otherwise the feedback is pointless, i.e., slanted too favorably for your personal development. Also, research has shown that the most accurate feedback comes from people who've known the feedback seeker between one and three years. The next most valuable feedback would come from people who've known the recipient for less than a year, followed by those who've known the recipient for three to five years. The least accurate feedback comes from those who've known a recipient for over five years. The reasoning is that those you seek out for feedback should have known you long enough to no longer be subject to first impressions but not so long that they've started to generalize too much in your favor and cannot be objective. In other words, don't ask your mom.

The High Cost of Low Status

"It's important to study power and status because hierarchy is everywhere. You can't get away from it," says Nathanael Fast. "Whether you're with family and friends, volunteering at a soup kitchen, or working in a big organization, there's always a hierarchy."

It's important because power can easily become corrupted, sometimes with devastating results. Fast, assistant professor of management and organization at the University of Southern California's Marshall School of Business, along with Nir Halevy, acting assistant professor of organizational behavior at the Stanford Graduate School of Business, and Adam Galinsky, professor of management and organizations at the Kellogg School of Management at Northwestern University, recently published their findings on the destructive nature of power in the *Journal of Experimental Social Psychology*.

"The world was shocked when pictures circulated in 2004 showing low-ranking U.S. soldiers physically and sexually abusing prisoners from the Abu Ghraib prison in Iraq," the study says. "One could point to these examples as support for the popular idea that 'power corrupts.'"

As more psychologists and business schools come together to study how power shapes business relationships, the researchers examined the interaction between power and status. Lacking status, the study's authors write, makes people feel disrespected and unappreciated. People will compensate with aggression to boost self-worth, the study says. "Considerable research has suggested that lacking status leads to violence. For example, children chronically rejected by peers are often aggressive, disruptive, and impulsive. Power has also been linked to demeaning and aggressive tendencies, with more power leading to more demeaning behavior."

In the case of Abu Ghraib, though prison guards had power, their roles provided little to no respect and admiration in the eyes of others. "They had power but they lacked status. We posit that understanding the combinations of these two variables—power and status—produces key insights into the causes of destructive and demeaning behavior," the study says.

We can all be high, medium, or low status in different situations. The trick is to figure out when to be what at the right time, and more important, how to use that status to get on the radar and create opportunities.

I'm reminded of a situation I observed at my hotel while on a recent trip to Singapore on behalf of Hewlett-Packard. I was there to conduct an Executive Presence program for the company's Asia-Pacific-Japan region management team. The concept of status differentials and how to navigate them was on the agenda for the morning. Having coffee at the lounge of my hotel, I noticed a visibly unhappy guest sitting on a sofa, with his luggage at his feet, ready to check out. An approaching manager, clearly aware of the guest's discontent, made the gesture of crouching next to the guest—one knee to the ground—and speaking calmly to him while in this decidedly low-status position. After a few minutes, the guest seemed to soften, with posture relaxing and facial expressions warming up a bit. A few minutes further into their quiet dialogue, a second, higher-ranking manager appeared, and while the first manager stood up and stepped back, the second manager got down into a similar crouching position to resume the undoubtedly apologetic theme of the exchange.

I imagined how the guest must have felt, having both these managers make themselves physically lower than the guest, and how different it would have come across had the managers remained standing—a high-status posture vis-à-vis the unhappy, sitting guest, looking right down at him while trying to convey their regret at whatever had transpired that soured his experience. The managers' social intelligence in adopting a more humble posture, to underscore that their mission is to serve the guest, saved the day. At the end of the exchange, the guest stood and smiled warmly and then enthusiastically shook both managers' hands. Well done, I thought, and a great example of how one can adopt certain nonverbal communication that conveys the appropriate status relative to that of someone we hope to influence. We can add this "situational status" to our toolbox of making a positive mark on someone's radar.

A Reality Check

As you're reading this, you are likely reflecting on your own relative status as well as that of the people in your immediate environment. And as we try to improve our position in the competitive struggle for rewards and resources—with a keen eye on the chance of getting on bigger and more important radars—we look to people who've made it to the top for inspiration. Certainly they can provide valuable lessons. Barbara Kellerman, the James MacGregor Burns Lecturer in Public Leadership at Harvard University's John F. Kennedy School of Government and author and editor of many books and articles on leadership, zeros in on how the well-connected can get on even more people's radar to create even bigger opportunities. Take Hillary Clinton.

A successful attorney in her own right, Hillary Clinton nevertheless took a back seat as First Lady when husband Bill ascended to the role of president. While he was in office, Clinton named her to head the Task Force on National Health Reform. Despite the polarizing effect of her proposed healthcare legislation as well as the subsequent scandal that nearly cost Bill Clinton the presidency, Hillary emerged triumphant. After her tenure at the White House was up, she became the first wife of a president to seek and win national office and the first woman to be elected to the U.S. Senate from New York. She was reelected in November 2006, but shortly after, she announced plans to run for president herself.

However, Kellerman cautions women who are looking to Hillary as a role model for seeking political office. "From day one she had national name recognition, coffers filled with money, and an experienced political machine—every one courtesy of her husband," Kellerman wrote in the *Harvard Business Review*. More than that, by bearing close witness to President Clinton's eight-year stint in the Oval Office, Hillary gained experience by association.

Not that there's anything wrong with that. As I mentioned in the previous chapter, one of the best ways to get on the radar is by leveraging your social networks to connect with as many influencers as possible. However, being realistic with the things you can accomplish with your own existing network will help you stay clear-minded and make the right moves as you decide on whom to approach for key stepping-stones.

Managing Your Status

If status is primarily something a group bestows based on personality, achievements, and a particular social structure, it's helpful for you not only to know your own status but to take stock of the power of those you want to impress. Once you're on their radar, they will be able to lend support, while their influence can improve the quality—not to mention frequency—of your opportunities.

Parsing this out can be as simple as drawing up a chart that prioritizes by power all the individuals who are interested in you and your work and are able to help you reach your goal—or at least have some influence over whether you are going to get there. For example, if you are angling for a promotion, your boss is most likely to have the power to influence that decision. A good leader develops other leaders, and if you're in the opportune position to work for one, put your boss at the top of the chart. Your best friend at work—a peer, for example—may be your biggest fan, but she can't make you vice president or give you a raise, and so she gets the bottom slot on the list. Other coworkers who can support you, and who may be able to provide the critical references you need to back up your bid for the better job, would go somewhere in the middle. Be particularly sensitive to the occupants on that part of the chart, as they can make or break your status at work. Team players are far more likely to be talked about in a positive way, something to keep in mind if your CEO spends any time at all around the proverbial water cooler with an ear tuned to the corporate grapevine. As Ken Caruso, vice president of human resources for S&P Capital IQ and S&P Dow Jones Indices, told me, "There is a formal narrative, and there is an informal narrative that exists in the executive corridor." It's important to keep in mind that the informal narrative has a tremendous impact on one's status.

It's likely you have a sizable list of people once you are done with this exercise, so the next step is prioritizing them according to how much sway they have over whether or not you reach your goal. Those whom you must engage with the most have both the power and the interest in your success. Peripherally high-powered individuals who are less interested should be less of a priority and not bombarded by your progress every step of the way. Those who aren't as influential also fall into two camps: very interested in your goal and less interested. You need to keep both informed and continue to communicate to make sure no problems arise that may stand in the way of your success. Understanding all these key players is a process, a dialogue in which you ask them about their personal views and motivations. Be sure to ask them what they think of your current status and work to discern if they are supportive. If not, ask yourself what you can do to change their impression of you. In the event you are unable to win them over, you must begin to build a strategy to deal with a potential opposition. These conversations have the added benefit of being good relationship builders, and gaining support later on depends on forming solid bonds.

Once you've asked the questions, be sure to note on your list who you expect to be an advocate and who might try to stand in your way of getting on the radar. That's the next step in managing these individuals and gaining their support.

All this will take time. Just how much time will depend on the scope and challenges of your project or goal, as well as how much time you have and how much assistance you'll need to get results.

Analyze the list of people and identify how much support you'll require each of them to provide and what you'll need them to actively do on your behalf. Next, you'll need to communicate exactly how reaching your goal will help make their life better. This is a good place for noting key performance drivers such as achieving a certain amount of market share or improving certain aspects of a current situation.

By encouraging an ongoing dialogue with these interested parties, you'll be able to stay on their radar and perhaps get on the radar of some others as a result. If something isn't going as planned, be sure to inform those who will be directly affected. It's better to get this out of the way up front. Everyone appreciates honesty and accountability.

In the next chapter we'll look at examples of finding common ground and explore how having interests in common can be a powerful way to get on others' radar.

CHAPTER 3

Finding Common Ground

Whener Harry Houdini was barely 20 years old, he discovered he was quite adept at slipping out of handcuffs and other types of shackles used to restrain human beings since ancient times. Unfortunately for Harry, no one cared. There wasn't much of a market for this kind of spectacle. To have a skill like that back then would be similar to developing a smartphone app in 2005—a full two years before the iPhone debuted in 2007. That's the challenge when taking on a new market: make or do something consumers are quite familiar with, and you'll have lots of competition. On the other hand, pushing something completely new will require you to establish its worth to everyone else—no mean feat. One way to make it easier is by cultivating common ground.

Sensing When There Is Common Ground: How Harry Houdini Got on the Nation's Radar

The crucial first step toward sparking the change you want to see in someone else's—or some group's—behavior is getting on the person's radar, drawing interest, and gaining standing in the arena of debate and action.

Average Joes and Janes need to step into the spotlight, even for a moment, and then make the most of the glow. Or if you are already in a high-powered position and are already on the radar, this step may be more about getting your issue or project on the radar, in the same way that celebrities championing social causes need to build a bridge from their current spot on the radar—that of entertainment—to the radar of, say, social justice or the antiwar movement.

Whether you're a celebrity, a CEO, or an everyday working stiff, you need to find common ground in order to get on someone else's radar. That's the overlap you share with the person or people you want to influence. Something in common will provide an "organic bridge" between you and your communication target. But it doesn't happen in a flash. Anthropologists studying a foreign culture can't just show up one day and say, "So, tell us all about your most secret rituals!" They often spend time, respectfully and humbly, around the people they want to study until those people decide they are comfortable enough to let the anthropologists "in."

Usually, though, if you look, you will find preexisting common ground. But my point is, you always have options. Like Harry Houdini.

Beyond his ability to toss off shackles, Houdini was a genius at looking around, spotting an existing region of common ground, and using it to get on the radar in a big way, incidentally and eventually making him a legend. Though this example is from another era and may sound like it's somewhat removed from the doings of your particular business, Houdini's ingenuity, colorfulness, and memorability make a great example that modern professionals can learn from.

Houdini's tale also incorporates other elements of the four-step process, including setting the agenda, making meaning, and sparking action. That's because real life is rarely so neatly compartmentalized as our framework might make it seem. In fact, when the great communicators and success stories do their thing in a memorable way, they usually have hit all four parts of the process, and hit them well.

But back to our hero. Houdini was born Erich Weisz in Budapest, Hungary, in 1874 and changed his name to Harry Weiss after his family immigrated to the United States four years later. When he later discovered the work of a great magician and conjurer named Jean Eugène Robert-Houdin, Harry Weiss became Harry Houdini, and the rest is history.

Well, not exactly. While there was a big appetite for amusements in the 1890s, there wasn't exactly a huge market for escape artists. If there had been, we wouldn't today know the name Houdini—we'd know the name of some other person who more or less invented the art of wriggling out of straitjackets and handcuffs for paying audiences.

So how did Harry Houdini manage to make escape art the object of national fascination? He had a brilliant marketing strategy for getting on the radar, built on common ground.

In the 1890s, cities in the United States were growing with amazing and sometimes frightening speed. They were places of industry, leisure, commerce, . . . and danger. Urban police forces were called upon not so much to investigate crimes but to keep cities safe and streets (relatively) free of hoods, thugs, thieves, cutpurses, and miscellaneous no-goodniks. In 1890, according to the U.S. Census, there were 82,200 arrests in the nation's largest city, New York. There were 48,119 in Chicago, the nation's second-largest city, and 42,673 collars in Philadelphia, the third-biggest city in America. No wonder there was a great deal of paranoia, especially among the middle class, that America's burgeoning cities were cesspools of criminal activities, with ne'er-do-wells flourishing like some nasty bacteria.

Houdini figured he would play to that paranoia. He found a compelling overlap—common ground—between his talent for getting out of constraints and something that was looming large in the national psyche: could police physically and metaphorically contain the crimes and criminals in their growing cities? A clever PR professional or guerrilla marketing effort couldn't have focused on a better issue.

Houdini decided to show that the police were largely inept at containing criminals. On November 22, 1895, he walked into a police station in Gloucester, Massachusetts, and "offered to escape from any handcuffs they could place him in," according to Houdini biographers William Kalish and Larry Sloman. The Gloucester cops took him up on the bet and lost—big time.

Houdini took off on a whirlwind tour of police stations in New England and eastern Canada, freeing himself from the best the constables had to offer. Now escape art was very much on the North American radar, and so was Harry Houdini. He soon became the first performer with a "dumb act"—that is, one that did not rely much or at all on speaking—to become a major headliner in variety, vaudeville, and music halls. From there, his legend only grew.

Harry Houdini was also setting an agenda by promoting the appeal of entertainment and by injecting meaning by use of a narrative: lone freak artist takes on the entire police establishment and wins. Certainly, he sparked action because people increasingly came to see him perform, making him rich and famous, and then he used that spark to modify and enlarge his talents. But the most important lesson here is that Houdini cleverly noticed what he had in common with what was going on and used it to grab the spotlight.

You don't have to be Harry Houdini to use common ground to get on the radar. But you have to be somewhat of a Sherlock Holmes to determine just what common ground you share with an individual or group whose attention you want to grab. We may work in someone's environment for years and yet be virtually invisible to the person, similar to the barista I mentioned in Chapter 1. Therefore, with colleagues, whether they are subordinates, peers, or superiors, try to determine their most precious values that you share and can tap into, in conversation or discussion, during a meeting, both informal and formal. Your approach to landing on common ground will be greatly enhanced when you know, for instance, that a colleague's top value is creativity—coming up with and trying out new ideas. What is it that you value in this regard? What common ground based on creativity is there to exploit to get on that person's radar? You will look for different common ground when you know that security—having steady employment—is a top value for a subordinate. Ask yourself how important this value is to you and whether there is common ground, and perhaps a personal story or lesson learned, that you can share to link to that person. Likewise you would modify your communication for common ground if you learned that your new boss's top values include having employees who work autonomously and with very little supervision. And if in turn your boss understands clearly that you most value receiving explicit recognition for the work you do, she can start relevant conversations from that basis from which more difficult turns in the conversation can follow more productively.

Additional ways to get on someone's radar include sharing challenges that others have experienced and sharing interests that you have in common, professionally or personally. Emerging from obscurity and onto someone's radar—whether it's a group or individuals—requires deep curiosity, detective work, and online research. You'll know that it has paid off once your desired target has become aware of you and the things you have in common and is interested in hearing from you and open to listening to your ideas.

Recognizing Dissatisfaction

It's no secret that many Americans struggle with weight. Suburban sprawl spawned a culture where it's common to spend a chunk of the day holed up in your car, driving between home and office, school and soccer practice, regularly scarfing down fat- and sodium-laced drive-through meals washed down with a side of sugary soda. Thanks to this turn in our culture, the Centers for Disease Control and Prevention found in 2009 and 2010 that 35.7 percent (more than one-third) of U.S. adults and 17 percent of children were obese. No wonder a weight-loss market, one that pushes everything from packaged food, pills, and powders to books and diet plans, is forecasted to hit $66 billion in 2013.

The ballooning obesity problem also provoked a backlash against the food industry. Consumers were becoming more aware of just how much high fructose corn syrup was in that 64-ounce Super Big Gulp and how many calories you would consume with that Double Quarter Pounder with cheese—750. (Still want fries with that? That's 500 calories extra if you order a large portion.) While sales at many chains were still soaring, there was an even bigger opportunity at hand. As Americans became more conscious of what they were shoveling in as they shuttled to work and school, why not put a new, low-fat face on fast food—one that's just like theirs.

Enter Hal Riney, the veteran advertising executive who masterminded iconic campaigns for Saturn cars, Bartles & Jaymes wine coolers, and the reelection of President Ronald Reagan. Riney stumbled across a newspaper article about a guy named Jared Fogle while working on a new marketing campaign for Subway's sandwich chain in 1999. Fogle's story began when he was just a 20-year-old junior at Indiana University and was regularly consuming 10,000 calories a day, plowing through pizza, French fries, and multiple trips to the Chinese buffet. Eating enough for five sent his weight soaring to 425 pounds. Fogle knew something had to give when his knees and wrists began to hurt even when he was sitting still. So he turned to fast food, again. This time, Subway came to his rescue, providing sustenance without a lot of fat. Fogle went on a strict diet of two subs a day and dropped a whopping 245 pounds.

Riney knew he had a winner on his hands. Weight loss tops the list of New Year's resolutions, and Fogle was a regular guy who slimmed down and stayed trim all by eating "fast food." Unfortunately, Subway wasn't biting. Fogle's story was interesting, but he was no actor. After refusing the concept three times, the chain finally agreed when Riney said he'd finance the ads himself. Success was almost immediate.

After the Jared spots ran in the Chicago–northwest Indiana area as a test, Subway called to ask if it could run the ad nationally. Sales shot up more than 20 percent. Since then, Fogle has appeared in more than 50 commercials and helped Subway to more than double its sales to over $8.2 billion.

Riney passed away in 2008, but Fogle is still going strong as the bespectacled face of Subway. The chain has tried other tactics, but it's hard to beat the fact that more than a decade after Fogle officially retired his fat pants, his likability and recognition rates are still high. In 2008, Subway was the second most recognizable brand behind Burger King.

A report in *Advertising Age* confirms what Riney instinctively knew. "Fat guy gets skinny eating fast food. It's irresistible," wrote *Ad Age* columnist Bob Garfield. "He's also an adequate presenter with plenty of personality and an easy smile. What he lacks is, you know, talent." Others have said that he appeals to women without being threatening to men and that he's not likely to be found boozing and womanizing at clubs. But Fogle defines his appeal best: "People relate to my story. They're very eager to say hi, they want a picture, they want to know that I did do what I said I did."

You don't need to study popular culture the way advertising executives do to capitalize on the real people driving (and buying into) those trends. But the idea—not to mention skill—of getting others' attention with something that resonates at a deep personal level, like an ordinary guy losing an extraordinary amount of weight without an expensive exercise program or esoteric diet, is one to remember and hone to a fine point. No matter what profession you're in, if you can authentically tell the story of someone "just like your audience" who benefited greatly from your idea, product, or service, you are resonating. If people believe you, you've provided a shortcut to their decision making, shown proof that what you offer works for people like them, and, most important, established yourself as a solution provider for their problems. Clearly an effective way to get on their radar.

Finding Common Ground in Divisive Times

There's an old chestnut that suggests in earlier days those in polite society refrained from discussing fraught topics such as money or politics at the dinner table. What happens now, in an age where the table is as likely to be your lap as you grab a quick breakfast on the way to work with your carpool or when your table mates number in the hundreds on your social networks? As social media encourages oversharing and the web is littered with sites that act as soapboxes for anyone with the money to buy a URL, your opinion—no matter how well researched or thoughtful—is likely to be met with an opposing view, or 50. Mix in a few hot-button issues that range from same-sex marriage and abortion rights to partisan politics, climate change, and evolution, and it's no wonder civil conversations often give way to combative, polarizing monologues pitting people on both sides as adversaries.

Unfortunately, our brains are hardwired to disagree with perceived opponents. As Thomas Leeper, PhD, writes in his blog *Polarized*: "We often think that the other side in a political debate is trying to destroy America, or at least offering a dangerous alternative to our own views of the political good. Often coupled to that skepticism of opposing views is an inability to understand how it is that our seemingly intelligent friends, family members, and acquaintances could hold political viewpoints that appear to contradict so blatantly with what we see as right." In other words, if you were using Facebook during the months and days leading up to the last presidential election, it's likely you came across status updates from "friends" who were quite vocal about their diametrically opposing views on who should lead the country. Whether you found yourself shaking your head, clicking "unfriend" to delete them from your network, or engaging them in a debate right on their wall, you've felt the tug of our basic human need to defend your views from threat.

That tactic isn't likely to win friends and influence others. What's needed (besides a deep breath and a giant step away from the megaphone) is an exercise in understanding the differing viewpoint and finding common ground.

That's exactly what Jonathan Foley, director of the University of Minnesota's Institute on the Environment, calls for in a piece on climate change in the Institute's magazine *Momentum*. Instead of stepping in the ring and putting up your dukes time and again, why not slip off the gloves by reframing the debate to highlight any area of agreement between scientists and skeptics. In an interview on NPR's *Talk of the Nation*, Foley explained it this way: "When you walk in, instead of saying you're the bad guy and I'm here to tell you what's wrong with you, if instead you say, well, how can I help your business be more profitable, how can we help America be more competitive, how can we make our country more secure, you go in as a friend, not as an, you know, opponent. And suddenly, the conversation changes, or you can have a whole new tenor to it."

Instead of communicating from our own perspective, we should always meet others where they are and take their beliefs, values, and experiences into consideration. It's the only way to eventual agreement; it's an immutable truth for getting anywhere in the world of work and business. Our office mates, business associates, and clients rarely start out as being our friends, and cultural and socioeconomic, not to mention hierarchical, clashes are all but impossible to avoid. Yet to succeed at collaboration and teamwork and organizational harmony for a common purpose, an open mind and respect for differing viewpoints are critical. Of course, the odds aren't always in our favor. Disagreeable behavior at work is often subconsciously rewarded, making win-win situations and the finding of common ground a bit more of a challenge, however worthwhile. That's because corporate hierarchy sets people up to behave badly, according to recent research. A 2011 study from the University of Notre Dame, which appeared in the *Journal of Personality and Social Psychology*, found that disagreeable people (especially men) earn more money and are perceived as better leaders.

Foley offers another example of finding common ground with people we don't necessarily choose to share space with. In this case, he was focusing on the differing opinions about global warming found in his home state of Minnesota. The state spends about $20 billion on energy annually, but because it doesn't have any naturally occurring resources like oil or natural gas or coal, he suggested thinking in terms of the local economy. Foley reframed a larger, polarizing conversation about whether or not climate change was affecting our environment as one that targeted how to keep that $20 billion from leaving the state of Minnesota. "I think when you approach people with those different kinds of angles to a similar kind of question, you suddenly can break the conversation open and, you know, really explore common ground, whereas just rehashing the same old climate debate again and again and again, just gets us locked in to somewhere we just never seem to go anywhere," he said.

No matter what the situation, you will discover that you have some common ground with your influence targets—other than the fact that you want something from them. This is not an artificial or forced scenario in which you make up something and awkwardly use it to build a bridge. Say you're gunning for a promotion that will switch you to another department. The catch is that your potential new supervisor is a well-known advocate for a product you believe has limited potential in the market. Otherwise, you've heard she's a nice as they come, and you really want that job. On the morning you cross paths in the coffee shop adjacent to your office, you have an opportunity to get on her radar. Instead of sucking up and pretending to be a supporter of product X, shift the conversation to trends you've observed in the marketplace while framing your own stance for product Y. This may make you uncomfortable at first, especially since you're not yet on her radar. Get comfortable with that discomfort. Not only will it pass, but it may yield an awareness of other ways you have something in common. And that is your starting point.

Practicing Empathy

Often, when people try to persuade someone, they tend to ignore the opposing viewpoint and fail to get on the person's radar in a positive way. Even President Obama recognizes this. In true diplomatic fashion, Obama asked Israelis to look at the world through Palestinians' eyes while urging enemies of Israel to change their rhetoric during a speech in Jerusalem. You can do the same in this exercise. Pick through some op-ed columns until you find a position on a hot-button issue that you agree with. It doesn't matter if it's about the size of sodas, climate change, illegal immigration, or the Israeli-Palestinian conflict, as long as you agree with the writer's take on the subject. Then consider the opposite point of view and write an argument for that position. As you draft your new stand, think about the views of your potential audience and see if you can find some overlap or common ground. Now go back to the original argument and revise the author's work, considering the opposing point of view and those areas of commonality.

Examining the opposing view leaves room to counter logically and get on the radar in a positive and constructive way. This is how you can learn not only to choose arguments but also to anticipate your audience's reaction and adapt to it. You now matter more. You have begun to engage, actively and conscientiously, in the first step of the breakthrough communication process.

In the next chapter you'll see suggestions for "hats" you can wear, or roles you can inhabit, to get on people's radar. There are many others to be sure, but the ones you'll read about should make you reflect on the varied ways we can get the attention of those we deem important to our goals.

CHAPTER 4

Nine "Hats" You Can Wear to Get on the Radar

U nless you were born into a royal family or a major celebrity's brood, you probably aren't a relevant fixture on anyone's radar, except your parents'. Take heart. Most CEOs, Nobel Prize laureates, political leaders, and Silicon Valley billionaires once walked among the unwashed masses, significant to close family members and friends, yet largely invisible to anyone else.

Getting the attention of any-size constituency often depends on the roles—professional and social—we choose for ourselves in life. So where are the opportunities for getting noticed as we go about our daily lives?

Here are nine ways, or "hats" to try on, to increase your visibility and inspire you to find your own opportunities for getting the positive attention of those around you.

The Contrarian

A noble, but tough, hat to wear. The main purpose of the contrarian is to go against the grain, but to disagree simply for the sake of argument merely makes you . . . disagreeable.

Contrarians perform a useful service, mainly by unsettling and forcing a rethinking of majority opinions or conventional wisdom.

They ask the questions others have long thought answered, and by doing so, they offer the possibility of new insights into old problems. Even when the answers don't pan out, shaking up the status quo compels individuals to sharpen their thinking to defend their own positions.

So how do you successfully cultivate the skills of the contrarian? Simply spouting off doesn't count. Neither does ranting, shouting, or in any way threatening others; these actions will only mark you as an ill-disciplined lunatic.

Contrarians are cool and levelheaded and are steeped in reason. If you've ever had the chance to see the late Christopher Hitchens in action, you've witnessed a master at work. Hitchens lived to puncture the self-regard of blowhards by speaking in a low tone at a fast clip, slinging arrows of approbation at their lazy thinking. He mustered vast amounts of facts and packed just the right amount of them like bullets into his rhetorical pistol. If he misfired on one shot, he always had another in reserve. Hitchens was witty and relentless, always moving, always thinking, the shark in the think tank.

The Hitchens approach is tough to duplicate, not least because his type takes on all comers at any time—a strategy that sometimes led him to overshoot wildly, not to mention it required extreme erudition. A more common and attainable degree is the contrarian who specializes in a particular field.

The education reformer Michelle Rhee is an example of this type of contrarian. She set herself up as a challenger to the education establishment and made a name for herself as superintendent of the Washington, D.C., school system. She appeared in *Newsweek* and was featured in the Oscar-nominated film *Waiting for Superman*, all to promote her quest to raise the standards of educational achievement by dismantling and reconfiguring the foundations of K–12 education.

Similarly, Steven Levitt and Stephen Dubner of *Freakonomics* fame applied economic analyses to problems and issues that had previously escaped the discipline of econometric modeling.

Rhee used her experiences to upend the thinking of the field in which she gained that experience, while Dubner and Levitt aimed their expertise outward, using the tools of statistics and economics to turn over the rocks in other fields.

A note of caution: Rhee and Dubner and Levitt have all been accused of misrepresenting their opponents, misunderstanding the dynamics of a particular issue, and mistaking their own righteousness for rightness. This can be a problem with contrarians. They're so eager to prove the other side wrong that they don't always take the care they need to prove their own arguments right. When people point out the problems with their own proposals, they may retreat into defensiveness, unwilling to engage on the very issues they themselves raised.

Still want to be a contrarian? If you want to be effective, cultivate knowledge in a particular field and critically examine the presumptions of that discipline. So much of the value of contrarians comes from their willingness to question assumptions, take little for granted, and grant little to others.

Your provocations will be taken seriously only if you take the topic seriously, that is, only if you're interested in more than scoring points. Not only know what you're talking about, but know the other side, too, and be prepared to follow through on the consequences of your questions. You can perform a valuable service to those around you, even if they don't always appreciate the pins you shoot into their hides.

EXAMPLES: Christopher Hitchens, Michelle Rhee, Steven Levitt and Stephen Dubner, Rupert Murdoch, Stanley Fish, Ayaan Hirsi Ali, Salman Rushdie

The Innovator

When I ask my clients how they'd like to be seen as part of their personal brand, most mention the role of innovator or pioneer.

Innovators don't necessarily play well with others because they are often single-minded in their pursuits. This plays a large role in how they achieve their goals. They narrow their interests in order to focus on their objectives and are unwilling to tolerate intrusions. A good idea matters, but discipline is key to developing that idea, a discipline bordering on obsessiveness.

While there are plenty of people who've invented groundbreaking devices or heralded a new approach to a phenomenon that no one even recognized as a problem, and who, by dint of bad timing, faded from history, there are plenty of others—from Newton and Edison to Tim Berners-Lee and Mark Zuckerberg—who've reached global acclaim and household-name status.

While being highly educated can't hurt, it is drive and passion that are the must-have traits of innovators. Sir Isaac Newton was considered an "undistinguished student" while at Cambridge, and he developed his theories on calculus in private study at home over the course of a couple of years. Thomas Edison, founder of General Electric and holder of close to 1,100 U.S. patents, lasted three months in an official school and was subsequently home-schooled by his mother. Most innovators have an intense interest in their subject. Steve Jobs began obsessing about computers while in high school, and upon dropping out of college, he worked in and around various computer-related fields, cultivating friendships with other computer geeks (including, Stephen Wozniak) before founding, with Steve Wozniak and others, Apple Computer. Apple, of course, pioneered the graphical user interface, setting a standard for ease of use among those not literate in programming code.

Bill Gates's early path into computers paralleled Jobs's, down to developing an early interest in computers, having friends who became cofounders of his company, and dropping out of college to pursue his interest in computers. (Mark Zuckerberg also created Facebook with friends and dropped out of college to tend to his invention, although his relations with his cofounders have been considerably rockier.) Nathan Myhrvold, cofounder of Microsoft, now heads up a company to support innovators and hopes to leverage invention into social and economic gains.

Not all innovators are as well known. Spencer Silver and Art Fry, both employees of 3M Corporation, are responsible for the now-ubiquitous Post-it notes found in offices everywhere. Silver had invented a low-stick glue but was unable to interest others in developing the product. Fry happened to have attended one of Silver's seminars. Then while in church battling an errant hymnal bookmark, he thought to put the glue on the back of the paper. Fry's "genius," connecting two apparently dissimilar things to fix a minor, but common, problem, led to the Post-it note, and history.

Innovation isn't restricted to science and technology, either. Ron Popeil took what he learned from the old boardwalk barkers of amazing! new! inventions! and applied it to the television audience. He's known for the Veg-O-Matic and Mr. Microphone and the Showtime Rotisserie, but his real innovation was in marketing. Taping a half-hour commercial in front of a live and appreciative audience led to the infomercial, while the thrill of time-sensitive offers of "absolutely free" widgets and gifts increased the number of sales.

Innovations in social practice are just as important. Bill Gates made his fortune as head of Microsoft, but he's now at least as well known for giving that fortune away through the Bill and Melinda Gates Foundation. He's among a crop of new philanthropists who've brought increased attention to accountability, attempting to ensure that his funding has maximal positive impact upon the foundation's chosen issues. Another social innovator is Nobel award–winning Muhammad Yunus, who incorporated the idea of microlending in his founding of the Grameen Bank, an institution that extends credit to impoverished and unbanked women.

You don't need to be a geek to innovate, and you don't have to go it alone. In fact, collaborators may be key in bringing your idea to fruition. Reflect on your passion, either within a particular field or for an entrenched problem. Or maybe you have a niggling irritation—like the bookmark that won't stay put—which you'd like take care of, once and for all. Either way, a passion to solve problems—or to create solutions to problems we didn't know we had—can catapult you to greater visibility.

EXAMPLES: Steve Jobs, Bill Gates and Melinda Gates, Nathan Myhrvold, Mark Zuckerberg, Ron Popeil, Muhammad Yunus

The Coach

He won 10 National Collegiate Athletic Association basketball championships, 7 of them in consecutive years. He led the UCLA Bruins to 4 undefeated seasons, through an 88-game winning streak, and compiled an all-time 40-season winning percentage. He coached Lew Alcindor (later, Kareem Abdul-Jabbar) and Bill Walton, as well as Jamaal Wilkes and Marques Johnson, among other eventual NBA players.

John Wooden knew how to coach and how to get on people's radar with his skill.

His approach was simple. He wanted his players to be in shape, to be quick, and to work as a team. Defense was a full-court zone press; and while he had nothing against dunks, if a player showed off, he was benched. Wooden was also strict and formal with his players, telling Bill Walton to cut his hair and informing other players who wanted to stage an anti–Vietnam War protest that if they missed practice, they'd be off the team.

Some appreciated his dignity even at a young age, while others chafed at his instruction. Abdul-Jabbar noted that Wooden called him Lewis, "a decision [which] endeared me to him even more. It was formal, my full name. I was no baby Lewie." Johnson, on the other hand, had little patience for his life lessons (Wooden's 15-block Pyramid of Success) when his mind was on more immediate pleasures. It was only after he got older that he realized how the pyramid could help him teach his own kids. Abdul-Jabbar observed, "He was more concerned that we became successful as human beings, that we earned our degrees, that we learned to make the right choices as adults and as parents. In essence, he was preparing us for life."

Pat Summitt, now head basketball coach emeritus at the University of Tennessee, does not enjoy the same mystical reputation as Wooden, but her reputation, especially among women basketball fans, is close to legendary. As a coach, she was known for her glare when upset, but like her predecessor, she was known for fielding both good ballplayers and good students. She passed Wooden as the all-time winningest NCAA coach and led the Lady Vols to eight NCAA championships—and counting. Just as impressive was her 100 percent graduation rate: she required her players to attend every class and to sit in the first three rows. Like Wooden, she had a formula for success (a 12-step list) that she applied to her own work.

Other coaches have won multiple championships, and others have sent multiple players on to the professional leagues, so what is it about Wooden and Summit that sets them apart and has others still take notice?

It's not just their dedication to the game. Both Wooden and Summitt began playing as children and worked their way up the coaching ranks. No one has ever accused either coach of slacking off or taking the game for granted. But the players commanded all their attention. They worked their players hard and demanded complete commitment to the team, a commitment they share. Of the Lady Vols' many successes, Summitt has noted, "The things I'm credited with are the result of a great number of others coming together to achieve goals they set together."

A good coach knows how to win. He or she devises tactics or recruits talented players. A great coach knows that winning is achieved by the people who play the game. You can easily see how this applies to teams anywhere, not just athletic pursuits. When you're a great coach, people outside the arena take notice.

EXAMPLES: John Wooden, Pat Summitt, Dean Smith, Phil Jackson, Joe Torre

The Networker

The playwright John Guare may not have intended to set off a social phenomenon, but his play *Six Degrees of Separation* sparked popular interest in the notion that a person might know someone through his connections to someone else. The parody *Six Degrees of Kevin Bacon* tries to link Hollywood players to Kevin Bacon through their connections with one another; it usually doesn't even take six steps. It was the social network before *The Social Network*.

You don't need an encyclopedic memory to network, but you do need to be social and to pay attention to the people you meet. Networkers are immensely important to almost any organization. Those who work in civic or humanitarian associations have to cultivate relationships in order to build that web of support. But networking goes beyond creating that web. It's about expanding it, constantly adding new members and then linking those members to one another.

We tend to think of networkers literally, as people who are prodigious users of social networks. In compiling its list of the most influential people of 2010, for example, *Time* relied heavily on

Twitter and Facebook statistics, a method that yielded Lady Gaga the second and Ashton Kutcher the third spot on the list of the most influential people in the United States—only Barack Obama scored higher. (Reporter Nate Silver noted the absurdity of a list in which Taylor Swift is more influential than Nancy Pelosi.) You can certainly move people by feeding them a constant diet of Tweets, but is the power in the person or the technology? Maybe both.

Furious finger action on a smartphone keyboard can surely raise your profile, but if you want to be more than a celebrity, you actually have to connect. Stanley Milgram established that it takes about six steps to connect strangers, which means that it doesn't take much to weave together millions and millions of people.

Do you know Lois Weisberg? Well, there's a good chance that if the former Cultural Commissioner of Chicago doesn't know you, she knows someone who knows you. Why? Because Weisberg is an inveterate networker. She didn't have a plan, but she collected people everywhere she went and then introduced those people to one another. She might have only passing acquaintance to someone, but that doesn't stop her from linking this acquaintance to another. She is an intensely social person who almost can't help bringing people together.

Visibility is key to getting on people's radar. Say yes to invitations to lunch and gallery openings and school fund-raisers and neighborhood events. Answer the phone and return calls, and don't be timid about ringing up someone you met at your son's track meet to ask if she was serious about wanting to teach a computer class at the local women's shelter. If you're sponsoring a blood drive, ask your network members to bring in their network members, and be generous about spreading the word of others' talents and good deeds.

It used to be commonplace that exclusivity was a mark of power. The key to networking influence, however, is inclusivity. You want to bring the world together.

Examples: Lois Weisberg, Reid Hoffman, Ariana Huffington, anyone who's ever succeeded in pulling together donors or volunteers or a group of semistrangers to fulfill a goal

The Power Broker

Discretion is the name of the power broker's game. He wields influence on the powerful and gains power as a result, but that doesn't mean he wants you to know who he is.

Brothers David and Charles Koch, for example, haven't necessarily been eager to wave the family flag. While David Koch has been a trustee at New York's Metropolitan Opera House, has given generously to theaters and museums, and has helped raise millions of dollars for cancer research, neither he nor Charles were particularly well known until recently.

The Koch brothers, in addition to running Koch Industries, have been funding libertarian and conservative political movements for years. They founded the libertarian Cato Institute, fund *Reason* magazine and the advocacy group Americans for Prosperity, and have been linked to the Tea Party movement. As oil refinery executives, they have also long lobbied against environmental legislation and pollution controls. They've poured hundreds of millions of dollars into political organizations and political contributions. They have worked assiduously behind the scenes to influence American politics and culture, much to the admiration of those who share their views.

For the moment, it seems the Koch brothers are becoming the biggest whipping boys for the left. An unflattering profile in the *New Yorker* seemed to break open a dam of pent-up progressive energy, and the Kochs' sprawling political and economic empire has been renamed the "Kochtopus." The brothers are no longer underground and just on the radar of an elite group of insiders. And though their wide-ranging money-wielding apparatus has been revealed, the Kochs haven't been rendered ineffective. Similarly effective in getting and staying on the radar are political operatives such as Karl Rove and K Street lobbyists such as Thomas Boggs of Patton Boggs. Both are well known and highly influential. So is George Soros, who for years has openly funded liberal and democratic causes in the United States and around the world through his Open Society Institute, and few would suggest his fame works against him.

There is something about the image of "backroom influence" that lends a certain mystique to power brokers. One way to cultivate your visibility and influence as a power broker is to keep to the back alleys of power. When an executive or powerful person asks for your counsel and discretion, you offer both. If asked by a bystander what you know, you smile enigmatically and say nothing.

Some power brokers achieve their position based on longstanding ties to a powerful person—Valerie Jarrett and Barack Obama, for example—so loyalty to a smart and ambitious person may pay off for you down the road. Others, like baseball agent Scott Boras or Hollywood agent Richard Lovett, represent and control access to players in their respective fields; and still others, like Tom Donohue of the U.S. Chamber of Commerce, gain their brokerage power through the firms they head. These power brokers variously know how to spot talent, apply pressure to friends and adversaries alike, and array institutional resources around a particular cause.

They gain influence and get on important people's radar by working through others, but even among those whom we do know, we don't necessarily know exactly how they work. Could anyone do what they do?

They're likely to smile enigmatically and shrug their shoulders. The mystique holds.

EXAMPLES: Charles Koch and David Koch, Karl Rove, George Soros, Scott Boras, K Street lobbyists, Richard Lovett

The Leader

It's easy to identify formal leaders: they tend to have titles such as president or prime minister or chief executive, and they often travel with a retinue of assistants, aides, advisors, and possibly a security detail. Most of us are unlikely ever to have retinues or even less formal entourages.

Leadership isn't about the office, but the qualities that allow someone to attain that office. Those qualities can be cultivated by even the most unlikely of candidates. Take Dong Mingzhu, president of the Chinese air-conditioning firm Gree Electric. Born the youngest of seven to a working-class family, she was a young widow and mother with neither wealth nor political connections. Dong was a technician in a Nanjing factory before heading south and landing a job as an air-conditioner saleswoman. After four years she was producing one-eighth of Gree's annual sales, an eye-catching figure that landed her on the radar of key decision makers, leading to a series of promotions. By 2001—just 11 years after starting at Gree—she was running the company.

Dong certainly benefited from a good relationship with her supervisor Zhu Jianghong, but once she ascended to the top, she adopted business practices unheard of in China, including charging retailers up front for merchandise and offering six years of free service to customers. She pays her workers above-average wages and gives them twice the paid maternity leave that other companies allow, all the while increasing Gree's revenues and expanding overseas.

How'd she do it? "You must be a thinker. Be decisive, have good judgment, organizational ability. Most importantly, you have to be able to take control," Dong said. And she never gives up. "I am willing to accept responsibility and meet a challenge. And I never compromise."

Leadership clearly requires organizational skill and a certain doggedness. Though vision is crucial for leading any organization, Dong built her vision along the way. She hadn't set out to take over an air-conditioning company, but once she had her opportunity, she capitalized on it.

Similarly, Jenny Beth Martin didn't set out to start a political insurgency, but inspired by CNBC's Rick Santelli's rant about the U.S. government bailouts and mention of a "tea party," Martin organized the nation's first tea party protest, in Atlanta. She spread her message via phone and e-mail and helped coordinate protests for the April 15 deadline for filing income taxes. The movement exploded, and she's now the CEO of Tea Party Patriots.

How did a homemaker and wife of a bankrupt businessman end up featured in a film about Tea Partiers and speaking at a national rally in Washington D.C.? Partly timing. Her political sensibilities and the national mood converged during tax season, and a wave of publicity (not all of it favorable) helped to propel her into the spotlight. "I never intended this," she has said. "I guess I just raise my hand too often and volunteer constantly."

It's also clear that Martin, like Dong, worked to take advantage of the opportunities that she had a part in creating. She didn't sit home and stew over politicians' actions; she got off her duff and made her views known. She worked to spread her beliefs, enjoying both the responsibility and the attention that comes along with it. Finally, her very ordinariness has worked to her advantage as someone who seeks to represent millions of regular-Joe Americans.

There is no magic to becoming a leader. There is only hard work, a focus on developing one's communication skills, a keen sense of self- and interpersonal awareness, the courage to make hard decisions, and the willingness to take the risks and jump through that window of opportunity whenever it appears. Chances are, it'll land you on important people's radar.

EXAMPLES: Dong Mingzhou, Jenny Beth Martin, Michelle Bachelet, Anita Roddick, Rahm Emanuel

The Expert

Want the influence that comes with being an expert? Develop expertise.

It sounds so simple. Find a vein and mine it, and don't stray into unrelated territory. Experts often benefit from people's erroneous belief that expertise in one area means they are knowledgeable in other areas too. But experts are rarely generalists.

Developing deep expertise takes time. People who have become experts in their fields tend to be older. Plenty of attractive and baby-faced "experts" appear on various cable news shows, giving their learned opinion on everything from financial advice to foreign policy to tissue reengineering. I suspect that most of us would rather see a gray-haired pilot steering the plane and an equally salt-and-pepper-topped neurosurgeon inserting a probe into our open brain when we're the passengers and patients.

Malcolm Gladwell said in *Outliers* that true expertise takes at least 10,000 dedicated hours to obtain, which would mean it eludes most people until at least their mid-thirties. You can't rush expertise, but you should steadfastly work on acquiring it.

Warren Buffett did not become the "oracle of Omaha" in his twenties, although he did begin his business career at a young age. At six he was buying six-packs of Coke and reselling the individual bottles for a profit. He kept his hand in business all through school, then worked his way up in brokerage houses in Nebraska and New York, eventually relocating back to his home state to start his own business. A career begun almost 20 years earlier began to yield enormous gains.

The enormous profits he reaped from his values approach to investing and his disinclination to join the latest financial fads gave him credibility as a financial sage. While he was derided for missing out on both the dot-com and subprime housing booms, the collapse of both of those markets only served to solidify his reputation.

Francis Collins, currently in charge of the National Institutes of Health and former head of the Human Genome Project, earned both a medical degree and a PhD in physical chemistry He was in his late thirties when he helped discover the gene for cystic fibrosis. In his early forties, he took part in the successful hunt for the genes for Huntington's disease and neurofibromatosis, among others. He was 50 when the rough draft of the human genome was completed, an event that helped propel him into the national spotlight. It was an ascent over 30 years in the making.

Both Buffett and Collins have offered their opinions on matters other than investment or gene hunting. Buffett has made known his skepticism of certain governmental policies, and he has served as an advisor to then-governor Arnold Schwarzenegger and raised money for Barack Obama's presidential campaign. Collins, on the other hand, has waded into the turbulent waters at the confluence of science and religion, writing a book and speaking out on what he sees as the affinity of these two oft-conflicted fields for one another. Neither of these men strayed from their original fields of expertise. They extended themselves, but they never let go of the anchors of their success.

Growing old is not enough to make you an expert (except in getting older, and perhaps not even then). These men dedicated their lives to a specific field and tilled it over and over until they amassed the knowledge and experience to give them credibility as experts. The way to gain influence as an expert is to develop expertise. Depending on how sought-after that expertise is, it can definitely lift you from the masses and onto the radar. But there are no shortcuts.

EXAMPLES: Warren Buffett, Francis Collins, Sonia Sotomayor, Richard Posner

The Writer

Amy Chua is a law professor and mother who recently wrote a book on raising her two daughters, titled *Battle Hymn of the Tiger Mother.*

Chua has a successful career at Yale Law School, but not until her book was excerpted in the *Wall Street Journal* did those outside her professional circle even know her name. Now she's known as the woman who ripped up a card her four-year-old daughter made for her as not good enough and who castigates American mothers for being too soft on their children. She has been interviewed on national radio programs and appeared on *The Colbert Report*—and not because of her professional accomplishments but because of the kind of memoir she penned about childrearing.

Whether Chua is able to sustain her visibility, the influence she has had on the national conversation over how to raise a child is anyone's guess, but she certainly made a mark in the cultural zeitgeist.

Others have established their cultural credibility over a much longer career. *New Yorker* writer Malcolm Gladwell has turned a number of that magazine's articles into bestselling books and helped to popularize such concepts as the "tipping point." He is the author of a profile of superconnector Lois Weisberg, has explored the role of the bar code in transforming mail-order business practices, and recently was one of a number of journalists looking into the question of long-term brain damage in football players. He's carved out a niche as someone who cocks his head at a situation, spots an overlooked opening, and then crawls inside to find out where this particular entry will lead. In typical counterintuitive fashion, Gladwell advocates for gaining expertise in a field outside journalism if you want to be a journalist. He said, "Aspiring journalists should stop going to journalism programs and go to some other kind of grad school. If I was studying today, I would go get a master's in statistics, and maybe do a bunch of accounting courses and then write from that perspective. I think that's the way to survive. The role of the generalist is diminishing. Journalism has to get smarter."

Tina Fey may be best known for her roles as a comedic actor, but writing is at the base of her success. She started writing while working in Chicago improv, created her own roles on *Saturday Night Live*, wrote and directed the film *Mean Girls*, and wrote for and starred in the television show *30 Rock*. She also published a bestseller called *Bossypants*.

Samantha Power is now known as an advisor to President Obama, but the Irish-born human rights activist cut her teeth in journalism. She was a war correspondent for a number of newspapers, later moving to long-form journalism turning out essays for weekly magazines and writing two books, one of which, *The Problem from Hell*, won the Pulitzer. Her work led her to a Harvard professorship and later to a position in the presidential campaign of then-senator Obama. Her writing about war and politics led to a career as an advisor on matters of war and politics.

J. K. Rowling went from being a single mom living on welfare to billionaire author named the "most influential woman in Britain" by a number of magazines, all after conceiving of the Harry Potter series on a bumpy train ride through England's countryside. Rowling leveraged her fame and wealth to become a noted philanthropist, supporting a number of prominent causes.

The common threads among all these stories? Some use their writing to advance their writing careers, and some use writing as a springboard to other activities.

If you want to get on the radar and create influence as a writer, you do actually have to write—and so it helps to know how to write. Some people have a natural facility with words. Even if you're not one of them, reading good writing and good criticism can help you to develop an "ear" for what sounds right. But there's really no substitute for plunking your butt in the chair and pulling out the keyboard or pen and paper and setting down the words. Writing is a skill that must be developed. The only way to do that is to keep writing.

There are few excuses for not getting your words out there. It costs nothing but time to start and maintain a blog, and local newspapers are often quite willing to publish editorials or analyses penned by articulate community members. If your company or organization publishes a newsletter, offer to pen a piece; and if your professional organizations maintain a website, contribute to it. If you want to be noticed by influential people via your words, then you have to get those words out there.

EXAMPLES: Samantha Power, Amy Chua, Tina Fey, Malcolm Gladwell, Jim Collins, J. K. Rowling

The Linchpin

It may have started in Tunisia, when a desperate young man set himself on fire. Or maybe it was in Yemen, where thousands turned out to protest autocratic rule.

Perhaps it began when Egyptian Google marketing executive Wael Ghonim created an anonymous Facebook page to commemorate the June 2010 police beating death of Alexandrian business owner Khaled Said. The page offered ordinary Egyptians their first glimpse into the widespread torture practiced by the Egyptian regime and became a rallying point for those protesting police brutality around the country. Ghonim posted videos and photos and constantly updated news and information on the site. His page, one activist said, was an "information channel" for protesters.

After Tunisians revolted, Ghonim announced the birth of Egypt's revolution, inviting his 350,000 "friends" to join him in Cairo's Tahir Square. Of those, 50,000 said yes. Uncertain that anyone would actually turn out, Ghonim worked with other activists to spread the word of the march on January 25. Two days after that first, successful march, Ghonim disappeared into the labyrinth of the Egyptian security apparatus. Others continued to use his Facebook page to rally supporters for an even bigger "day of rage" protest. When the government shut down the Internet, activists resorted to phones and word of mouth to bring people out.

Ghonim was released 12 days after his disappearance and soon was interviewed on satellite TV. He insisted that the men and women in Tahir Square wanted only their rights and dignity, stating repeatedly, "We are not traitors." Upon being shown the photos of those who had been killed during the protests, Ghonim broke down, blaming authorities for their unwillingness to relinquish power. Less than a day after the interview, 130,000 people joined the Facebook page titled: "I delegate Wael Ghonim to speak in the name of Egypt's revolutionaries." A retired army general stated that the interview revealed a truth long suppressed by state media.

Wael Ghonim was a linchpin for the Egyptian protest movement.

He wasn't the first to criticize authoritarian rule, nor did he single-handedly summon tens and then hundreds of thousands of Egyptians into the streets. What he did do with the Khaled Said Facebook page was to create the crossroads where different interest groups—the seasoned activists, the newly engaged, and ordinary citizens—could meet, share information, and decide on how to act. He wasn't interested in leading the revolution, but he did want to lead others to the revolution.

You can't necessarily plan on becoming a linchpin. This role usually combines skill, position, and serendipity. Based on prior work he had done with Mohamed ElBaradei and his efforts at democratization, Ghonim saw the power of social media as he came into contact with other like-minded Egyptians. Ghonim was perfectly positioned to respond to the beating death of a countryman, and using his skills as a marketer for a social media company, he marketed the truth of Said's death.

On the other hand, some people are able to identify the vital nodes in an organization—the budgetary office, say, or operations—and maneuver themselves into locations through which all significant information, decisions, or resources must flow. A supply sergeant in the army, for example, exerts a great deal of influence over who gets what and when—a firm position on a lot of people's radar.

The bottom line is that if you're able to locate the choke points of your organization, you can become a critical player in the lives of everyone within it and leverage the resulting influence in your favor.

EXAMPLES: Wael Ghonim, Malala Yousafzai, Lech Walesa, Mark Felt aka "Deep Throat"

This is only a small sample of the types of influential roles you can inhabit in order to get on others' radar. You may find that one or more of these hats fit your natural inclinations and proclivities or that you'd like to further develop one of the areas. Your goals should be to self-reflect and find the place where you can start developing and profiting from increased visibility in order to move to the next step for a successful breakthrough communication process.

Now that you have some sense of why one needs to get on someone else's radar and how to do it, beginning with Chapter 5, we move to the second step in the process: introducing the specific topic or topics you wish to see addressed, in other words, making your ideas salient and establishing the agenda.

Step Two

CHAPTER 5

Setting the Agenda: Focusing on What Really Matters

ow that we've covered in detail the important first step of getting on significant others' radar, it's time to introduce the idea of *salience-agenda*. Basically any time someone opens his or her mouth in the presence of another interlocutor, the struggle begins for establishing salience for any particular issue and establishing the agenda. Tune in to any station on the radio or TV at any time, from ABC News to Charlie Rose to Fox and MSNBC, and the salience-agenda is often immediately apparent: essentially whatever is being talked about.

You could, of course, also be standing in line at the grocery store and see the phenomenon in action: Shopper #1 is going on about the outstanding curriculum and faculty at the $30,000-a-year preschool at which her kids are spending the mornings, while shopper #2 offers some stats she's read in *O* magazine that show that kids benefit more from spending that time around family and friends in a less structured environment. Plus it's a lot cheaper, adds #2. For shopper #1, who appears to be flush with money, the salient point is an early start into education, while shopper #2 makes salient the idea of family time as proper nurture for the little ones. And on a whim, either could try to change the topic—or agenda—to gossip about common friends, speculate about why there's a lack of female directors in America's corporate boardrooms, or debate the merits of stay-at-home dads. The possibilities are as endless as the mind can dream up, and either party—more or less successful in taking equal turns—engages in salience making and agenda setting.

The media—different from us mere mortals—with every channel we are tuned to, has the overwhelming power to determine the topic, choose the guests, ask the questions, slant the meaning, add music for effect, determine the camera angles that infer meaning, control the time, select (or withhold) the evidence and show it on-screen, cut people off, etc. The same goes for any of the opinion-driven mass media, like newspapers, magazines, and websites. Outside of media, we can consider the next level of issue salience-agenda—setting power, such as that of powerful, well-funded organizations like lobbying groups and associations that can wield great power over decision makers and anyone else who should listen to—and adopt—their agenda.

It's easy to see how salience-agenda is typically controlled by those with resources and those in power. This book, however, is primarily for those who aren't in power and don't have access to virtually unlimited resources. I am trying to teach those who need to achieve breakthrough communication on a "small budget" how salience-agenda is created for a greater purpose, to level the playing field a bit. In the course of history and the annals of business, there have always been individual actors and advocates for causes or change agents who established salience-agenda with their issues in spite of being an underdog. In this chapter I am determined to make the concept of salience-agenda superclear in all its simplicity. It's important to note that the process of creating salience, or setting the agenda, is ongoing. This provides both opportunities and obstacles: the media can highlight a crisis or a trend—which means you can take advantage of the attention—but in doing so it means you'll have to compete for the interpretation of that event.

Recognizing Opportunities

Okay, now that we have a clear picture of what salience-agenda means and how it can be achieved for breakthrough communication depending on your rung on the power-influence ladder, we will learn about recognizing opportunities. Here I want to look primarily at two types of opportunities: one is a "focusing event," and the other is "in the air."

Focusing Events

Social scientists talk about "focusing events," meaning those phenomena that rivet everyone's attention. Political scientist Thomas Birkland defines a focusing event as "an event that is sudden; relatively uncommon; can be reasonably defined as harmful or revealing the possibility of potentially greater future harms; has harms that are concentrated in a particular geographical area or community of interest; and that is known to policy makers and the public simultaneously." He and other scholars research the impact that natural and other disasters may have on the policy-making process, in particular, how such focusing events create openings for activists and skeptics of the status quo to push their agendas. He notes that "focusing events can lead interest groups, government leaders, policy entrepreneurs, the news media, or members of the public to identify new problems, or to pay greater attention to existing but dormant problems, potentially leading to a search for solutions in the wake of apparent policy failure."

This might appear to contradict Richard Vatz's perspective of salience and agenda, but it actually complements it: a focusing event is a fusion of the sudden appearance or occurrence of such event, with interpretations of that occurrence. It is something to which people pay attention because the media and credible sources guide us toward salience: they interpret the event as something worth focusing on. Common types of focusing events in politics and business include a hurricane hitting a major American city, an undersea earthquake and a resulting tsunami swamping a nuclear plant in Japan, the threatened collapse of an economy's financial sector, mergers and acquisitions, leadership scandals, product recalls, etc. Advocacy groups that are dissatisfied with the status quo point to these events as exemplifying the failure of current policy, and they push for changes that will, they believe, mitigate the effects of or prevent future similar situations. They're not always successful—those who favor the status quo will push back, and advocates compete with one another for primacy in setting a new agenda—but the breakdown of the old order does create an opening for change. Keep in mind that a situation doesn't *create* rhetoric, but rather how (and what) we choose to talk about the situation gives birth to an agenda by making an issue salient.

None of these focusing events actually determine the rhetoric (per Vatz), but rather the rhetoric created the perceptions taken in light of the various components of the situations, whatever they might be. The point is that a focusing event can open the door to salience-agenda making.

An obvious example of a focusing event in recent times is the Boston Marathon bombing of April 2013. This horrific act of anonymous terrorism was carried out at a major sporting event where there was sure to be not only a traditional media presence but hundreds of people with smartphone cameras to help document the scene and focus the country's attention on it, if not the world's attention. As it turned out, the bombing was carried out by two brothers who were immigrants to the United States; were of Chechen origin (a central Asian Islamic culture); were to some extent interested in jihadist radicalism; were also apparently small-time marijuana dealers; had, it seems, learned bomb-making techniques on the

Internet; were in possession of at least one handgun; had largely grown up in a middle- to working-class suburb of Cambridge, Massachusetts; and had been left on their own as young adults when their parents moved back to their native homeland.

Now, no sooner did the first of these pieces of information begin to settle into place, than different voices in the public sphere and the media immediately began to wrangle over how it was most important to frame this tragic occurrence in the context of ongoing political debates, because it turned out to sit squarely at the intersection of an incredible number of these debates: gun control, immigration, Internet content regulation, drug enforcement, funding for public education, freedom of speech and religion, parenting and responsibility—you name it. Voices on the right were inclined to frame the incident as calling for stricter immigration controls, tougher penalties for marijuana dealers, a strengthening of family values, and a more robust effort to assimilate and Americanize immigrant children in our schools. Voices on the left were more inclined to frame it as highlighting a need for stricter gun control, legal rather than illicit marijuana sales, multiculturalism to make immigrants feel more welcome and at home, and more funding for public education and programs that might have helped to keep these young men from ending up so alienated from mainstream society.

In the Air

Another kind of opportunity presents itself "in the air"; this occurs when a variety of background factors combine to prime an audience for a particular message or product. Malcolm Gladwell has famously talked about a *tipping point*—that "one dramatic moment in an epidemic when everything can change." Similarly, the term *meme* is used to identify a particular concept that spreads in the culture; some memes leave few ripples behind, and others go viral and may become entrenched. When I say something is "in the air," I'm referring to that moment *prior* to the tipping point or the entrenchment of a meme, when the culture is ripe for a change that hasn't happened.

This is tricky territory. It's easy to see in hindsight what led up to a breakthrough moment, but how do you know ahead of time when the stars are aligning in your favor? Scholars of agenda setting have tended to focus on media effects. Maxwell McCombs and Donald Shaw, in their classic 1972 article on media influence on voters, "The Agenda-Setting Function of Mass Media," noted that voters correlated strongly with mass media's definition of noteworthy issues; follow-up studies indicated that, in fact, the media did not merely correspond to but *set* the agenda. Chris Vargo is among those attempting to adapt this theoretical concept to twenty-first-century media. He notes that while some studies indicate that social media venues such as YouTube and blogs follow mainstream media, others suggest a dynamic wherein the consumption of social media affects mainstream media, which in turn affects social media. In other words, the process of interpretation and agenda setting may become more fluid, insofar as more communicators have the opportunity to create and put their own spin on events.

Still, what happens *before* the agenda is set? In some cases, it's the vision or persistence of a single or a few actors that creates a new agenda. There seems to be an inchoate sense that something is about to happen. This may easily result from the circulation of similar memes, from a number of actors with similar ideas all competing to put forth their ideas, or from a long-standing problem or issue that receives media attention, any or all which may combine to ripen the cultural moment. This links up to Gladwell's notion of *contagion*, the time prior to the tipping point during which an idea or practice spreads among a subculture before breaking out into a wider culture. Publicity about a contagious practice can handily serve to prepare the expectations of a wider audience for a breakthrough—meaning that the ability to identify a potentially contagious practice can give you a head start in taking advantage of it.

"Change of Any Sort"

Just as we should be aware of the myriad opportunities to get on someone's radar, there are, of course, opportunities for creating salience that spring up in everyday situations. These are the kinds of chances either that one gets on an ongoing basis (weekly meetings, regular interactions with supervisors and colleagues, conferences) or that might arise out of the blue (the chance encounter with a leader in your company or field, a temporary assignment in a different department). These everyday opportunities may themselves arise in response to focusing events within your company or field or from the underlying corporate culture—you run into your CEO on the elevator, a new manager wants to reorganize departments, or management decides to turn its focus from, say, hardware to software or from business-to-business sales to retail sales—and as such provide you with the chance to put your agenda out.

The key here is to keep your senses sharp and your awareness pointing outward as much as inward. As I mentioned in Chapter 3 on common ground, opportunities can spring quickly, or they can form slowly, like vapor taking shape. If, for example, a business associate is working on an interesting new project that promises to lead to bigger opportunities, suggest collaboration, if you have the expertise and time. If you learn of a problem facing your boss that few others know about, consider ways you may help and offer to do so discreetly. If a competitor is encroaching on your particular market niche and you have an idea to position your firm better, do the research and make a solid case, but then be sure to speak up. The possibilities are endless, and as you can see, they are not just for those who already have power and a major voice or platform.

Establishing salience-agenda can be attempted by anyone, as long as the person has "source credibility." To do so, however, you have to make an impression. You have to *stand out*. When opportunities present themselves, whether suddenly or gradually, others will be competing to put forth their own ideas. To play and succeed, credibility is crucial.

Competencies to Help with Source Credibility

Psychologist Laura Belsten, who is part of our coaching team at GuruMaker, has developed a proprietary assessment—the Social + Emotional Intelligence Profile (SEIP)—for measuring one's emotional intelligence quotient. This assessment instrument is divided into four quadrants: Self-Awareness and Self-Management (Personal Competence) and Other Awareness and Relationship Management (Social Competence). The SEIP is a highly sophisticated assessment tool, one that depends upon 26 different competencies to build a profile, showing areas of strength and areas for development. Your credibility, in other words, depends on more than just integrity and initiative; it also depends on your ability to relate to others and other competencies that can aid in breakthrough communication.

The competency of Communication is about listening and about sending clear messages to others. People who have this competency are good with give-and-take; they listen well and notice the little things; they can deal with difficult issues; they like to share information; their speech is logical and organized; they aren't afraid of public speaking; they don't get defensive; they can deal with both good and bad news. People who don't have this competency, on the other hand, are often overly critical, so that other people avoid them; they are harsh and insensitive; they don't always consult enough with others; they are set in their ways and talk down to people.

You can develop the competency:

○ By teaching yourself to be positive with people in word and deed
○ By looking for ways to connect
○ By giving people space
○ By asking questions that aren't always either-or
○ By trying to grasp others' points of view

The competency of Interpersonal Effectiveness is about being in tune with the needs of others, making them comfortable, being courteous, and having mastery over one's self-presentation in social interactions. People who have this competency are savvy about social scenarios and the unspoken messages involved in them. It is important to really be interested in the people one is dealing with and to get a sense of what is going on inside their minds. That means you really have to be able to listen well and pay attention to what goes unspoken, too. It's crucial not to prejudge or interrupt the person you are speaking to, and its best to use open-ended questions in conversation. You have to be on the same wavelength as whomever you're dealing with in a given case. You have to pay attention to body language. Sometimes there are ups and downs in a relationship, and you have to be able to roll with them. And sometimes there are possible misunderstandings that arise from differences in identity, be it cultural, gender, religious, or socioeconomic. In some instances you have to give a little information in order to get some, and in other cases you have to be able to accept that people just have different styles of communicating. A positive attitude is key here, as is the ability to show other people that you get it. At times this can make the difference between succeeding and failing to overcome tensions in a relationship. People who don't have this competency often just can't relate to others and tend to seem cold, standoffish, and insensitive. They may seem to give insufficient respect, which is crucial. They may seem bossy or just clueless.

The best ways to develop this competency are:

○ To give people your undivided attention
○ To really try to see what makes them tick
○ To take one of several different kinds of personality test yourself, to come to greater self-knowledge
○ To seek sincere feedback from friends
○ To read and study up on interpersonal relationships
○ To notice how people normally react to you and see if you can figure out why

The competency of Powerful Influencing Skills is about effective persuasion. People who have it are able to bring others around to their way of thinking. They can tailor their self-presentation to their chosen audience. They can build consensus, often by being a little strategic in going about it. They can make great use of the narrative (see Chapter 10 of this book). People who don't have this competency are loners and often find themselves at odds with others. They don't make a good impression. They can't make their point of view appealing. They are clueless about knowing their audience, and they can't even defend their ideas effectively when these are questioned. They don't fill their listeners with confidence, and they may even seem boring.

The best ways to gain this competency are:

○ To always keep an eye out for opportunities
○ To read and study up on strategies of persuasion and influence and to have discussions with people who are knowledgeable in this area
○ To be an attentive, active listener

- To always think about what degree of dominance or status it is best to take on in a given interaction
- To understand and skillfully address people's motivations
- To strive for clarity in your communications and put the necessary time into planning and thinking about these in advance
- To think about how you want to spin or frame your idea and how to introduce it in a given conversation
- To think about what objections someone might realistically have to your point of view and come up with some ways of answering these
- To be on top of all the facts and statistics that you need to argue your side of an issue
- To know your area well enough to think out loud about it, which gives people confidence in your sincerity

The competency of Inspirational Leadership is about being able to lead people to your desired outcome. People who have this competency can use words effectively and generate excitement in others. They can unite people rather than divide them. They can rise to the challenge of leadership even when they have not previously been in a prominent leadership position. They can foster a feeling of community, a sense of emotional attachment among people. They can shake things up and introduce new ways of doing things. They can give people a sense of shared goals. People who do not have this competency are often vague in their ideas about the future or what they want to achieve. They focus on the "little things" and not what really matters. They don't manage to connect with others at a deep level, and too often they end up unnecessarily in conflict with other people. They fail to take into account how other people can offer huge advantages and not just obstacles in trying to achieve something. They can be judgmental and underestimate the importance of coalition building.

The best ways to develop this competency are:

o To think hard about the future
o To put your thoughts into words that are inspirational
o To not be afraid to think outside the box
o To use creativity and try to see things in a new light whenever possible
o To come up with new ideas
o To think hard about leadership and contemplate examples of it that are personally meaningful to you
o To get other people's input and let them take some credit for things that are accomplished together
o To take the long view and not try to control every little thing
o To give people some slack if they know what they are doing
o To always mind the example you are setting and to carefully protect your reputation for upright behavior, knowledge, and integrity

The competency of Catalyzing Change is about showing initiative and being the spark that sets things in motion. People who have this competency see when something new is needed. They are able to step up and take responsibility and figure out what needs to be dealt with. They are not intimidated by the resistance they may encounter from people who are more set in their ways. They are able to be an effective spokesperson for their point of view and to get other people on board with it through persuasive argument. They are able to set an example for others. They give people the "heads up" that they need about whatever is happening, and they show flexibility and adaptability. People who don't have this competency are content to just accept their lot in life, and they may not see a need for change even when it is staring them in the face. They keep on using the same old language, the same terms and phrases that are locked into the old way of thinking in a given context. They may be afraid of change and drag their heels against it in both obvious ways and more subtle ones. They don't plan carefully, and they don't keep an open mind.

The best ways to develop this competency are:

o To shake things up when possible
o To keep an eye out for possible improvements
o To paint a picture for others of what the advantages of change are going to be (this can't be stressed enough!)
o To put ideas clearly in writing so other people can follow your road map for change
o To keep people on board by maintaining their excitement and connection with your project and celebrating each of its little victories

The competency of Intentionality is about taking purposeful action and being strategic to reach your goals. People who have this competency are able to be decisive but also consistent. They are able to stay focused. They keep their cool and do not easily lose their patience in the face of adverse circumstances. They have clarity about their aims, both long term and short term. They can take responsibility for enacting their plans. People who do not have this competency are not good at setting realistic goals. They let themselves be passively affected by circumstances. They get distracted and sidetracked. They are unclear about what they want. (It is like the old saying, "If you don't know where you want to go, you are going to end up somewhere else.") They don't plan ahead sufficiently to achieve positive results.

The best ways to gain this competency are:

o To really search your soul about exactly what it is that you want, both short term and long term

- To let it be okay for you to have dreams and pursue them
- To open up to people in a real and genuine way
- To stay focused and plan ahead
- To get help when you need it
- To believe in yourself

The competency of Innovation & Creativity is about openness to new ideas and ways of doing things. People who have this competency are not afraid to look around for new ideas. They think outside the box. They are focused on effective problem solving. They know how to ask questions and get people's minds working. They are able to take risks when appropriate. They are able to throw off the old, stale assumptions that may constrain the thinking of others. They keep an open mind and are versatile. They are able to maintain a positive mental attitude toward what may look like failure at the time but is really an opportunity to move in a new direction. People who don't have this competency are overly fretful and can't cope in a dynamic way with changed circumstances. They have a tendency to be negative about things, to take a "glass half-empty" perspective. They can be complainers rather than doers. They are stuck in their ways and reluctant to try out things that are unfamiliar.

The best ways to develop this competency are:

- To be in touch with your creative potential rather than just your analytical side
- To be able to brainstorm productively
- To think hypothetically and imaginatively about all sorts of possibilities
- To know when to take a break and give yourself the rest you need to function effectively
- To make sure your physical environment is clean and comfortable and not distracting

○ To be able to follow up any new interest that presents itself
○ To imagine what somebody who is your *exact opposite* would do in a given situation
○ To look out for things that surprise you

The competency of Initiative & Bias for Action is about taking charge and following through. It is about seizing the moment. People who have this competency are active rather than passive in pursuit of their goals. They give the proverbial 110 percent and go beyond the call of duty. They don't let petty obstacles get in their way. They know how to make effective use of the skills and energies of other people. They make sure to take the initiative in any fluid, dynamic situation. Generally speaking, they want *more* out of life. People who do not have this competency tend to drag their feet and lose their way. They need to be managed by somebody else. They don't like to go outside their comfort zone or their narrow "job definition." They are reactive rather than proactive, which means they are always playing catch-up with the world. They are often quitters. They are not very good at making plans, either short term or long term. They let chances go by through a timid and hesitant approach to life.

The best ways to gain this competency are:

○ To have a "get-it-done" mentality
○ To set realistic goals and carry them out
○ To just get started rather than waiting for all conditions to be perfect first
○ To have a "can-do" attitude
○ To "seize the day!"
○ To think about what might be impeding your progress both externally and internally and to deal with whatever ambivalences may be getting in your way
○ To divide up your time into chunks for set tasks

○ To do the hard part first, whatever it is, so the rest of your task will be smooth sailing

The competency of Realistic Optimism is about having the right attitude and expectations, looking at the positive side of a situation to see the possibilities in it. People who have this competency are able to see beyond immediate, short-term obstacles. They know the power of positive thinking and speaking. They really believe in themselves, that they *will make it happen,* not just that they can or could. They are consistent in acting on this principle. They are able to free themselves from the shackles of fear. They see a connection between success and hard work. They know that setbacks are inevitable but can be overcome. They take everything in their stride and see adversity as opportunity. They redouble their efforts. They don't "blame the victim" when something goes wrong but realize, instead, that sometimes stuff just happens. According to empirical research, these people live longer, healthier, happier lives than anyone else. People who don't have this competency are pessimists. They see setbacks as expressing the ultimate truth about them as people. They tend to just give up when the going gets tough. They can suffer from poor mental and physical health. They see themselves as passive victims in life, and they don't believe that skill and determination can bring success.

The best ways to gain this competency are:

○ To think about how you frame the world to yourself in your private thoughts and in the language you use
○ To really think about how you deal with adversity, intellectually and emotionally
○ To challenge the tendency toward self-doubt if you find it within yourself
○ To strive for objective evidence that things are not as bad as you might have feared them to be

The competency of Resilience is simply about "keeping calm and carrying on." People who have this competency can recover quickly when they face setbacks. They have often learned effective coping strategies in the course of their lives. They know how to optimize and leverage their resources. They have a cheerful attitude toward life's little stumbling blocks. They know that failure is a *temporary* and not a permanent condition. People who do not have this competency get "stuck in a moment," just as they tend to be stuck in a rut and set in their ways. They use a lot of negative language with others and with themselves. They always see the downside.

The best ways to acquire this competency are:

o To live *healthily*
o To rest and refresh yourself as much as is necessary to get through difficulties and challenges
o To change your vocabulary from negative to positive in emphasis
o To get in touch with your core values and insights
o To keep your eyes on the prize and see the light at the end of the tunnel
o To stay connected with others, be it friends or family
o To read stories and biographies of real-life people who have overcome adversity and dealt successfully with setbacks

The competency of Teamwork & Collaboration is about being able to work effectively with other people to bring about common goals. People who have this competency, first of all, *enjoy* working with other people. They know how to bring people together and get them on board. They have an instinct for team building. They give everyone a stake in the success of a given enterprise. They are open in their communications, and not secretive. They are generous. They know how to put the group's interest before their own. They work well with many different kinds of people, regardless of differences in personality or style. They show respect and build trust. People who do not have this competency are frequently introverts. They often shirk or shy away from responsibility for their share of a team's objectives. They are sometimes less than open with others. They can undermine the group behind its back. They are often conflict averse, with the result that issues don't get worked out. They think it is a hassle to have to work in collaboration. They don't uphold the team's standards and protocols. They constantly second-guess group decisions.

The best ways to gain this competency are:

○ To look for occasions when you can work collaboratively
○ To really try and see things from other people's points of view
○ To try to understand how you can be helpful to people in a given situation
○ To communicate clearly and openly
○ To be forthcoming with the resources as well as the assistance that people indicate they need from you
○ To give credit where credit is due
○ To be consultative rather than simply directive in your managerial style
○ To hold back a little bit and try not to dominate every discussion or planning session
○ To address conflicts head on
○ To show respect all around, building a bond of trust through honesty, sincerity, and ethical behavior

In the next chapter you'll learn about the importance of clarifying your purpose and the need to stay keenly focused on the specific outcome you're seeking.

CHAPTER 6

Clarifying Focus and Objective

We've all attended events where one person monopolizes the spotlight to tell a story about, say, her completion of a nightmare project. We might even jostle our way forward so we can watch her reenact going through the recycling bin to find that crucial missing file. Other times we edge away—subtly, so as not to offend—from a recitation of the minutiae of this or that business meeting only the storyteller could care about. One person is a raconteur, able to mesmerize us with humor, suspense, and consequence, while the other is a blowhard, boring us with details that matter to no one else but him. They both seek our attention, but while we gladly give it to the raconteur, we go out of our way to avoid the blowhard.

What do the raconteur and the blowhard do differently? The raconteur knows which details to emphasize and which to leave out, while the blowhard or the person who drones on and on (and on and on . . .) can't be bothered to shape his story or point his presentation in any particular direction. The person who knows what to do with the spotlight, in other words, is the person who knows how to streamline a story to keep his audience interested and to bring it to a conclusion we can all understand. He knows the importance of *focus* and *clarity* in leading to his objective—be it to entertain or inform us.

Making sure others understand your purpose is vital in the aim to have them embrace your agenda. Getting on the radar is the first step, but to really make your issues salient and your agenda impossible to ignore, you have to distill it all down to its compelling essence. Details matter in the follow-through, of course, but in presenting your ideas you have to keep those details from cluttering your agenda or otherwise distracting from your focus. In the following pages we'll have a closer look at the basics and importance of focus and clarity to advancing and solidifying your agenda.

The Art of Creating Focus

Say you have no trouble speaking up—a prerequisite for making *any* issue salient—and you're able to get the attention of people who matter. Based on your elocution, do those people know what you want? Are they clear on what you have to offer? Is your objective evident from the get-go? A crucial element in establishing your agenda is making sure that its various parts all point in the same direction and that nothing extraneous is included. If you want to accomplish A, don't wander off into the fields of P, Q, or Z.

Obvious, you might think, but what happens all too often is that people who are given a platform to advance one agenda will suddenly "discover" a facility for oration on a wide variety of topics.

Tempting as it may be, "Oh, as long as I've got you all here. . ." is a slippery slope that may end up derailing your best efforts at bringing an important issue to light and putting it on the agenda of critical things to consider. Ron Ashkenas, managing partner of Schaffer Consulting, observes that "one of the tough truths of management is that we all have trouble making choices." There's so much we want and need to do that "we proliferate products and projects and programs and proposals—each one of which makes good sense by itself, but in the aggregate overwhelm us, our organizations, and our customers." He notes that some of the biggest corporations, such as Pfizer and ConAgra, found renewed success when they pruned their organizations and cut back on product offerings, and he quotes GE's chief learning officer Susan Peters, who advises that "prioritization and focus are keys to doing well. Sure there are other things that are not on the priority list, but you do them differently or more slowly." This focus on, well, focus, applies as much to a high-stakes hallway conversation in the executive corridor as it does to global business strategy.

THIS Inc. CEO Greg McKeown notes that success can sometimes breed distraction: once we've achieved success, we have more opportunities, which can, in turn, lead to more distractions, which result in losing focus. Wandering down the alleyways and side streets might be great in the brainstorming phase, but once you've created your agenda, you need to keep your focus on that agenda and avoid getting sidetracked. Business consultant Dr. Timothy Bednarz advises managers to set clear objectives to motivate and direct their employees: "Detailed objectives keep managers on track and alert to potential interferences that can be addressed early before they create serious problems." The focus provided by the manager helps to maintain productivity and "allow managers to concentrate on future opportunities and establish new goals as future needs occur."

Special interests is a term many Americans learn in the context of power, politics, and big business. Those promoting said special interests are often highly effective persuaders, aka lobbyists. The job of a lobbyist is all about getting others to sign on to an individual's or group's agenda. Former legislators often become lobbyists, having established their credibility in a particular sector, not to mention that as former legislators they're already on their former colleagues' radar. Other lobbyists achieve their success due to their ability to bring their expertise on a particular topic to an officeholder, walk him or her through the "significant" issues, and suggest talking points, as well as legislative or regulatory changes, thus making decisions easier for the decision makers. One lobbyist for a trade association in London argued that "what I and similar people in other areas do is essential—you're providing MPs [Members of Parliament] and Peers with specialist knowledge to enable them to see the ramifications of the decisions they're making." American League of Lobbyists president Paul Miller echoes this sentiment, noting that, given the breadth of topics on which members of Congress legislate, it is unrealistic to expect them to know everything they need to know.

Regular citizens might not like the access that lobbyists have to officeholders, but legislators and bureaucrats often use them to provide information they don't have the time to gather for themselves. In fact, legislators are almost always short on time, so a lobbyist who wants to be an ally (instead of a pest) can do so by staying focused on particular objectives and making sure her agenda is in sync with that of the legislator. That, in the end, is the mark of a truly successful lobbyist: getting the legislator to adopt her agenda as his own.

Once you've clearly established the purpose of your agenda, a useful strategy would be to invite others to suggest other venues in which your agenda could be useful—this being an important part of buy-in, to get others to adopt your agenda as their own—and as it is implemented you might see fit to adapt your agenda to the changing circumstances. McKeown, who noted that the opportunities that success brings can lead to a loss of clarity, doesn't really counsel against exploring those other opportunities; instead, he emphasizes that if you want to avoid the pitfall of distraction, you have to double-down on your focus and double-check that those new opportunities fit *within* your agenda. It's a balancing act: you don't want to get sidetracked, but you don't want to get stuck, either. As Bednarz notes, establishing your focus at the outset will make it easier for you to maintain control and provide a touchstone as your agenda evolves.

Achieving Total Clarity

While we'll analyze the making of meaning via specific language in depth in Chapter 9, I'd like to focus on clarity in language specifically here, I hope without redundancy.

We'll take our inspiration from the philosopher Arthur Schopenhauer: "One should use common words to say uncommon things."

Using common words can be necessary in delivering vital information. Dr. Noni MacDonald and reporter André Picard, writing in the *Canadian Medical Association Journal,* lead off their editorial on vaccine safety with a quote from Albert Einstein: "If you can't explain it simply, you don't understand it well enough." They note that clear language has been important in obtaining consent for vaccinations, but "little attention has been paid to the same need for clarity in the language of scientific reports and academic articles." Because so many laypeople now have access to these reports, they might mistake the methodical language of "null hypotheses" and probabilities to reach a conclusion opposite from what the authors intended: "Such serious misunderstandings, whether by health care workers, community members, politicians, or journalists, can lead to widespread community belief that the vaccine in question is unsafe." They urge, "Academic jargon that obscures meaning must be replaced by crisp, understandable conclusions"—conclusions that can save lives.

On a somewhat less dire note, Dillon School District Two director of technology Paula Yohe bemoans widespread ignorance on information literacy standards. Among the causes of this ignorance is the unclear meaning of the term *information literacy* itself. "If you ask someone outside the library profession for a definition of information literacy, they often cannot provide a clear explanation. There needs to be clearer, universal terminology that can be easily defined and understood by others outside the library world." She notes that various literacy organizations have their own definitions, which increases confusion and leads to inaction: "If all educators and administrators are not clear on what information literacy means—and why it is so important—it is less likely to get noticed." Until these organizations can agree upon a common definition with a common set of standards—until they clarify their purpose—they will have difficulty convincing decision makers to implement their proposals to meet those standards.

In both cases, unclear language impedes the agendas of the respective advocates, either in misleading an audience about results or in failing to convince the audience of the issue's salience.

There are other ways to dissipate the strength of your message. A common method is to "go long": use as many words and syllables as you can possibly cram into one breath. Instead, follow the advice that one journalism professor at the University of Wisconsin posted on his door: "Eschew obfuscation"—always useful advice to anyone who might be tempted to believe cleverness matters more than clarity.

That professor apparently followed the line laid down by novelist and essayist George Orwell. In his famous *Politics and the English Language*, Orwell identified a number of problems plaguing his beloved language: dying metaphors (clichés), operators and verbal false limbs ("going long"), pretentious diction (fancy words or foreign phrases), and meaningless (dishonestly used) words.

While he put forth his rules for writers, Orwell was interested principally in thought: clear words indicate clear thoughts. Similarly, the late scholar Tony Judt cautioned that "when words lose their integrity so do the ideas they express." Both men lamented the way language was misused by politicians in order to mislead the public, but their admonitions extend beyond the political into *every* arena in which ideas matter. To state this more positively, if you want people to follow you, you have to state clearly where you're going. Words to live by for any breakthrough communicator.

How to Be Clear with Numbers

In his widely acclaimed book *Calculated Risks,* German psychologist Gerd Gigerenzer observed that even when we're as clear as possible, our audience still might misunderstand what we're saying. He looks in particular at the use of frequencies and probabilities in risk communication and how often the person hearing the information will take away an entirely different meaning from our presentation than what we intended. He gives the example of a psychiatrist who, in prescribing the antidepressant Prozac to his patients, informed them they had a 30 to 50 percent chance of developing a sexual dysfunction. While he meant that of every 10 people who took Prozac, 3 to 5 would have a sexual problem, they heard him say that they would have problems in 30 to 50 percent of their sexual encounters. "For years, my friend had simply not noticed that what he intended to say was not what his patients heard."

Gigerenzer traces these and other problems with numbers back to what John Paul Paulos calls *innumeracy,* or the inability to think with numbers. While innumeracy is similar to problems with unclear language—an inability to think with words—the solutions are not necessarily the same. If you are conveying information about risks, for example, it is important to stress that nothing is certain, and teaching people how both to ascertain risk and to be aware of what might impede their ability to do so is critical.

One colleague—a college professor—takes care in her classroom to note the slipperiness in risk communication. "Saying a practice triples your risk sounds daunting—but if the risk was only 0.3 percent to begin with, tripling it still leaves you at less than 1 percent risk."

Because numbers are often seen as "hard" or "set," it is easy to mislead, either intentionally—Gigerenzer offers a chapter on "how innumeracy can be exploited"—or without awareness. Shipping out 25 units of Product X in a year sounds like a fairly low production number, unless Product X happens to be an aircraft carrier. Similarly, doubling a city's population is much more impressive if that population grows from 5 million to 10 million than from 5 to 10. Thus, provide context to your numbers, whether in comparing your product with similar products, in putting a time frame around your production numbers, or in giving the absolute number and not just the rates.

Confirmation of Understanding

You've established your focus, eschewed obfuscation, managed the potential to mislead with numbers, and otherwise made your agenda as clear and understandable as possible. So how do you know if it worked?

Whether you speak in words or numbers, you have to make sure that you'll meet the people in your audience where they are. If you've been working on a project for some time, it's easy to forget that not everyone is as familiar with the issue as you are.

So where do you start? You start *before* the beginning, when you craft your message. You've set an agenda in response to some perceived problem or issue you want to address; reflect on and reiterate what it was that prompted you to think of change in the first place. If you're a public health physician, for example, you don't want to focus your message on the need for basic language on vaccine safety; you want instead to focus on the idea that illness rates have increased in areas where vaccination rates have gone down. If you're a game developer, you want to tell potential investors about the possibilities opened up by mobile apps. If you want to sell lessons in statistics, explain the problems caused by innumeracy. In every case, you want your audience to know where you're coming from.

Second, explain how you are using terms, especially those that might have more than one meaning or that have meanings that might be obscure. (Even after following Orwell's advice, you might still end up with terms with multiple or unfamiliar meanings.) Good teachers and professors are able to integrate such explanations into their lectures without condescending to their students. They might say, "While [this word] has multiple meanings, I'm using it to denote X," or "While [this word] is commonly used in another field, here's how it applies to our situation." In both cases, they're able to convey the definition while respecting the intelligence of their students.

Similarly, if you are talking to people outside your field, culture, or even generation, you want to make sure that terms that are common to you are understood by them. Take these three possible scenarios of misunderstanding: (1) Efficiency in drug delivery in the body doesn't mean the same thing as efficiency in beer delivery to grocery stores. (2) Referring to the USSR and Soviet Union and Russia interchangeably will likely confuse a classroom filled with students not yet familiar with the history of the Cold War. And, of course, (3) football in the United States has little in common with the more literally defined sport of football that's played most everywhere else in the world.

Then there are acronyms. Adam Gopnik offers a cautionary tale of not assuming you know what they stand for. In exchanging messages with his son Luke, he thought the term *LOL* meant "lots of love" and used it as a sort of "electronic hug" to reach out to those who were going through a bad time. It was only six months later that his son, noticing the odd inclusion of LOL in various messages, asked him if he knew what it really meant: "laughing out loud." Not exactly the appropriate response to news of, say, a divorce in the family.

Fourth, have a number of different ways to explain your agenda, since not everyone understands everything in the same way. Some people understand matters visually, some through metaphor, some theoretically, and others through concrete examples. One person will want you to lay everything out in charts and graphs, while another person might just want you to "bottom-line it for me." Because I want to reach as wide an audience as possible in my books, I use different explanations to illustrate the same underlying point: political examples fascinate some and frustrate others, and corporate examples don't necessarily work for the entrepreneur. If I'm speaking before a particular audience, I'll make sure to draw my examples from their field of expertise or greater industry, even as I mix up the way I present that information.

Finally, encourage feedback. The best way to know if people get what you're saying is to ask them if they understand. If not, ask a series of follow-up questions to elicit where the breakdown in communication occurred. Use different examples, illustrate your point dramatically, or word things in the language they can understand most clearly. In all cases, convey to your listeners both your confidence in your agenda and your eagerness for them to share in its purpose.

In the next chapter we'll look at how we can make issues salient when the odds and environment are against us. Where Chapter 5 showed us how to take advantage of various external opportunities to create salience, Chapter 7 will show us how to influence the agenda when the odds are stacked against us on our way to breaking through to others.

CHAPTER 7

Making New Ideas Salient

You may still think you have to wait for the right set of outside circumstances to come about for you to make your play, to raise your topic, to make your innovative ideas known. Not so. (Though if local or world events are relevant, so much the better.) Remember that *Breakthrough Communication* views you as an *active player*.

In Chapter 5 I highlighted agenda opportunities you could take advantage of; in this chapter I discuss how you can create your own agenda. This is arguably more of a challenge, as you have to overcome obstacles—be they apathy or outright opposition—in order to make yourself heard.

From Bare to Fertile Ground

Sometimes the best way to take advantage of an opportunity is to make it yourself. In Chapter 5 I noted that some opportunities are *in the air*, but others have to be pulled *out of thin air*. No one and nothing else will smooth the path to your agenda, so you have to take charge and lead the way yourself.

Birth of a Social Movement

Bringing an item into the conscious awareness of those around you, no matter if they're relatives, superiors at work, club members, committee colleagues, or even an entire nation, can require a single-mindedness familiar to the driven, the ambitious, the successful. We know the stories of this or that visionary who just kept pestering a person in some position of authority to try a new idea until the authority figure finally said, "All right, go ahead! Just leave me alone already." From such nagging are great innovations often born.

One individual who got on the agenda in a remarkable way in her day, one who changed the way we think about the world and its citizens, was Jane Addams, one of the national—actually international—leaders of the social reform movement.

Addams was born in 1860 in Cedarville, Illinois, the sickly eighth of nine children of a prosperous miller, John Huy Addams. (He was also a state senator, Civil War officer, founding member of the Republican Party, and friend of Abraham Lincoln.) Jane had a number of health problems, including a congenital spine deformation that made it hard for her to keep up with other kids and their activities. She managed to graduate from a women's seminary in 1881, the valedictorian of her class; and she even attended medical school for a while but dropped out due to poor health. She traveled, poked around for something to do with her life, and was finally inspired when, on a trip to England, she visited Toynbee Hall, a kind of charitable institution with outreach programs for the poor in London's East End.

That was it. With a clarity of purpose she had hitherto lacked, Jane Addams decided to pour her efforts into starting a similar "settlement house" in an underprivileged neighborhood in Chicago. Two years later, in 1889, Addams, along with confidante Ellen Gates Starr, left the safety and comfort of her home and moved into a large house "in a blighted neighborhood" on South Halstead Street in the Windy City. Before long, Addams and Starr were providing a vast range of much-needed services to some 2,000 individuals, many of them children, each week. Hull

House, as her institution was known, offered classes for children and adults, a public kitchen to feed the hungry, tradecraft instruction, an employment bureau, a swimming pool, and many other facilities for the support and enrichment of people in need.

But Jane Addams did more than provide a myriad of services. She put a new idea—or perhaps it is more accurate to say, a new twist on an old idea—in the nation's head: people with more means actively serving those with less. By her actions, as well as her notable speeches, writings, political stances, and other efforts in the public arena, Jane Addams forcefully advanced the idea that the better-off and the less-well-off did not inhabit two utterly distinct and unbridgeable worlds. "Hull House had as its main objective introducing middle-class individuals to the life of the urban poor," writes historian Bruce S. Jansson.

In other words, she put the notion of direct social service and empowerment on the agenda. It may seem far afield, but what can be learned from Jane Addams's promotion of social betterment for the poor is this: with clarity of purpose, one can feel confident taking a chance by delving into new frontiers that at first may seem alien. Not surprisingly, in 1910, she became the first woman ever to be awarded an honorary doctorate by Yale University. Twenty-one years later, in 1931, Jane Addams won the Nobel Peace Prize.

You don't have to be a Jane Addams to get your idea on the agenda. But it helps if you are clear in your purpose and are willing to delve into new realms. Indeed, the basic paradox about making a change or a difference, whether in your company, your business unit, your neighborhood, or even your family, is that if something has never been done before, it might just be considered "weird," i.e., not worth trying. But without trying to do the "weird" thing, the status quo will prevail. Jane Addams was willing to land in the middle of a neighborhood that most genteel folks in her day would never dream of setting foot in. But she literally settled there (hence the name "settlement house"). Eventually, through great toil and commitment, the suffering underclasses became more than just a concept—and one to be avoided at that—in the eyes of some in the middle and upper-middle classes. Indeed, thanks to Jane Addams, they became a little more of what they had always been, simply human beings in need of a little help.

How AMP Put Globalization on the Agenda and Never Looked Back

In the mid-1950s, American industry was on a roll. Flush with innovation from wartime advances and provided with an expanding peacetime market, companies were in a good position to make big profits and grow considerably, if they knew what they were doing.

One such organization was called Aircraft-Marine Products, soon to be known by the shortened moniker "AMP." AMP had been founded in 1941 by a former Westinghouse engineer with the memorable name Uncas Whitaker. Whitaker realized that there was need, especially in boat and aircraft manufacture, of a quick, easy, and reversible way to connect electrical wires without soldering, a "common thing done uncommonly well." He thus came up with a short metal tube with a ring on the end that could be quickly and easily crimped with the help of a small, scissorslike handheld tool that AMP eventually called "The Champ." (And if you didn't have one, the right pair of pliers could do pretty much the same thing.) Electricians loved it. Soon the United States was embroiled in the Second World War, and companies like Boeing and Ford needed to do lots and lots of electric crimping. They turned to AMP, and the company flourished.

With the war over, a number of companies that had been reliant on defense contracts faced tough challenges. After all, who needed, say, twin .50 caliber machine guns or a submarine periscope? Some companies—notably German ones like Porsche and Volkswagen—went from making tanks and troop transports to selling nifty roadsters and cheap runabouts. Others started acquiring competitors or diversifying, in so doing taking on debt and getting into areas where they lacked expertise. But AMP's products were so simple and adaptable to a range of electrical and electronic applications that the company did not have to reinvent itself. What AMP did have to reinvent was its market. The Big Three automakers, which should have been AMP's big customers, had set up their own supplies, essentially locking AMP out of the U.S. market. Whitaker responded by putting a bold issue on the agenda—one that seems so common to us now but in the 1950s was risky at best, a cultural anathema at worst—going totally global.

Mind you, AMP didn't merely set up shop in England or Australia (though it did that). It went right into the heart of lands that had been, until fairly recently, enemy territory: Italy, Germany, Austria, and Japan. In fact, during the 1950s, while American companies were aggressively selling their goods domestically and beginning to move into overseas markets, AMP actually set up subsidiaries in foreign nations staffed and run almost entirely by locals. Rather than colonizing these new realms, it more or less partnered with entrepreneurs there. In 1992, James Marley, who had been AMP's chief operating officer at the time the company was setting up its global operations, remembered a foreign customer saying that his company bought many AMP products and liked the fact that he was patriotically buying locally. When Marley said he worked for AMP in America, the customer said, "Oh, I didn't know AMP had a U.S. subsidiary."

In terms of accomplishing a goal of eventually selling more products and broadening its markets, AMP had gotten on the radar by virtue of its wartime contracts and its products' convertibility to peacetime applications. The agenda item it placed on the table, however, was the idea of going global: more than simply selling *to* foreigners, AMP was committedly and consistently selling *with*. "You can't be successful without manufacturing and engineering in a country," said then-chairman and chief executive

Harold McInnes. "We've gone [to new markets] with AMP people in the states and gotten things rolling. Then we bring in people from the country and turn the management over to them."

During the early 1990s, when other companies were suffering in the wake of a major recession, AMP continued to grow. By 1994, AMP had 185 facilities operating in 36 countries; that year, only 42 percent of its sales came from the United States; the rest came from Europe and a growing Asia-Pacific market. By this time, AMP was the market leader in a field with no fewer than 800 competitors (it was later acquired by Tyco for $12.2 billion).

Whitaker created the foundation for this success not just by producing a quality, in-demand product, but by expanding his vision beyond the domestic marketplace. Consigned to a corner of that market, Whitaker determined instead to move AMP into the world—and onto the global agenda—not just through engaging in trade but also by becoming an organic part of business operations in countries across the globe. The result of this strategy was that it paid handsome dividends—and an unintended result was that it established a business model copied by other companies that wanted to prosper as AMP did.

You might think, "What's the big deal? AMP just decided to open factories and sales departments overseas and, boom, success followed." In fact, AMP was taking a chance at a time when there was deep suspicion in the United States of foreign partners, not only for political and cultural reasons but also in regard to standards of training and infrastructure that were so unpredictable and varied. AMP did not have to make a big argument—to its investors (it did not go public until 1956) or to government regulators—and therefore it did not need to focus much effort on meaning making as per our four-step process. It did, however, have to take a chance. And though the decision may have looked strange and risky to observers at the time, nothing legitimizes an agenda item like success. You don't have to be a giant industrial corporation to get an idea on the agenda. You can simply voice what you believe in. And even in the face of doubt, trust your intuition. And keep at it. Eventually, what once seemed like a strange new idea will be one that others will copy, as if it had been like that all along.

Locked Out

If there are times you can set your own standard, there are others when the standard has already been set—and locked into place. In these cases you have to find a way into a market or a conversation where current players are determined to keep you out. The status quo works for them, so be prepared to weather their assault on your ideas.

No Monopoly on God

The Christian church began as a small sect within Judaism, then became a target of the might of the Roman Empire, triumphed over that same empire, and proceeded to spread over the whole of Europe. While the church split in the eleventh century into what is now known as Orthodoxy and Catholicism, Rome's dominance over the spiritual lives of Western Europe remained intact.

Not that this was an untroubled dominance. Princes and kings squabbled with the Catholic Church over control of lands and taxes; cardinals battled popes; and as education spread, so too did ideas critical of the way the church ruled over its parishioners. Various reformers challenged the church's authority, but even amid the turmoil, the center held: the would-be reformer Jan Hus was burned at the stake, and John Wycliffe, who had managed to die before he could be punished, was later declared a heretic and his body dug up and burned.

The Catholic Church was in charge.

So it had no particular reason to worry when yet another disgruntled theologian made public his dispute with what he considered the more odious practices of the church. On the last day of October 1517, the scholar-priest Martin Luther hammered into the door of the Castle Church in Wittenberg 95 theses on the reformation of a corrupt institution. In particular, Luther went after the sale of "indulgences"—a promise of forgiveness of sins in exchange for a "donation" to the church. Although a longstanding practice, Pope Leo X and the Holy See pushed hard for contributions in order to renovate St. Peter's Basilica. And although Frederick III of Saxony (also known as "Frederick the Wise") outlawed the sale of indulgences in his territory, the faithful would often travel to pay for their sins; upon their return, they could claim to their priest no need for further earthly discipline.

This completely unhinged Luther—a man not generally known for his gentle temperament—and is widely credited with pushing him into open criticism. The Holy See initially ignored the challenge, but as the theses were copied and widely distributed, it ratcheted up the pressure on Luther to recant. The "good monk," however, wasn't remotely inclined to back down, even after the pope issued a papal bull (public decree) in 1520 declaring Luther's works heretical and demanding he recant; when he didn't—in fact, Luther burned his copy of the bull—in 1521 Pope Leo X excommunicated him. At his trial later in the year before the Holy Roman emperor Charles V, Luther is reputed to have uttered the famous statement, "Here I stand. God help me. I can do no other." The emperor responded by condemning Luther as a heretic, and while honoring his promise of safe conduct back from the trial, the emperor nonetheless declared open season on the obstreperous monk, putting his life in danger.

Luther, however, benefited from the protection of Frederick the Wise, who, while a devout Catholic—he later became a Lutheran, albeit not publicly—protected his subject from both the pope and the emperor. As Luther gathered followers, the territory now known as Germany was thrown into turmoil. When, in 1529, Charles V attempted to expand his religious authority at the expense of German princes, they protested the move—thus leading to the term *Protestants*. Initially meant to disparage the dissenters, *Protestant* was eventually picked up as a term of pride by other dissenters and challengers to church authority, and what began as an attempt to reform the Catholic Church became a movement away from it, a movement now known as the Protestant Reformation.

Martin Luther shows it is possible to make headway against a dominant force—although not without a great deal of risk. He was not the first to raise questions about the authority of the church, but Luther was among the first generation of dissenters to finally crack open what had seemed an impenetrable lid smothering any public expressions of dissatisfaction. What he had going for him was a distracted leader, who did not immediately act against him, and a formidable ally, in the person of Frederick the Wise. He was also able to exploit the political conflicts between the emperor and various princes, some of whom sided with Luther in defiance of Charles V. Finally, Luther had a devoted following who not only protected him from kidnapping (and worse) but spread his ideas across Europe. Today, while many firms welcome suggestions for change and innovation, others operate as did the medieval church: while you won't lose your head if you challenge the status quo, you might lose your position. If you are determined, however—if you feel "Here I stand. I can do no other"—then before issuing your challenge, it is arguably a smart idea to ally yourself with a powerful person in your organization, as well as to cultivate your colleagues. Even if they don't agree with you, you want them to respect you for your integrity and be willing to defend you against attempts to treat you as a heretic. Who knows, maybe you'll end up leading your own reformation.

Thirsty for More

Americans like to drink beer; in 2009, U.S. consumers drank over 20 gallons of beer per capita. That's a lot of beer.

Most of that beer is made by the Big Two—Anheuser-Busch InBev and MillerCoors. These two megacompanies control 90 percent of the market, but smaller brewers, called "craft" brewers, are fighting to get their beers in front of more and more drinkers. (Post-Prohibition regulations set up a distribution regime that the macrobreweries have come to dominate, which means smaller brewers may have difficulty even getting their products on store shelves.) Some of the larger craft brewers, such as Samuel Adams and Sierra Nevada, now sell nationwide, but as more craft brewers have entered the market, there are continuing, often bitter, conflicts over the dominance of the Big Two as well as increasing tensions between the larger and smaller craft brewers.

One brewery, however, has decided to compete by *limiting* where it sells. New Glarus Brewing of Wisconsin not only doesn't market to the entire country; it doesn't even distribute its beer to neighboring states. The small-town (population 2,172) brewery is run by Dan and Deb Carey, who have stopped selling their beer in Illinois and now sell exclusively to their fellow Wisconsinites. If you want to try their flagship Spotted Cow beer, you'll have to travel to the Badger State for a pour.

Dan Carey started working in the beer industry in his early twenties, and after earning a bachelor's degrees in food science, he traveled to Germany to apprentice with a small brewery before returning to the United States for a few more apprenticeships. He'd worked his way up to production supervisor at Anheuser-Busch and was one of the few Americans to pass the Master Brewer's examination when, with the help of his wife (who raised the start-up money as a gift), he decided to go off on his own. While Dan toils with the copper kettles and the hops, company president Deb (the first woman in the United States to cofound a brewery) runs everything else, down to designing their whimsical labels.

So how have they managed to thrive in a state that built its reputation—the major league baseball team of the state is called the Brewers for a reason—on the Milwaukee-based macrobreweries? I should mention that it helps to confine your beer business to a state whose citizens really like to drink beer—over 36 gallons per capita (sixth highest in the nation). Still, the Careys did a great deal "backward." For example, while they do market their product, instead of "pushing" their beer to customers, they use the beer to "pull" the customers toward them, brewing a variety of beers and letting the customers decide which ones they like. They also *shrank* their distribution, deciding in 2002 that the expense of trying to distribute beer in Illinois wasn't worth it. "It caused quite a hoopla when we pulled out of Illinois," Deb said, "and it angered the wholesaler, but I didn't have a problem with it. My loyalties have always been to Wisconsin." The local-loyalty approach has also had the effect of pulling Wisconsinites toward this home-state brew, as well as attracting out-of-staters who travel to New Glarus for the brewery's weekly tours and, of course, some beer to take back home.

And as much as Deb Carey insists they focus on the manufacturing of their product, she and Dan do cultivate that local market. They urge their customers to "drink indigenous," and Dan has worked with area farmers to grow hops and barley for the company. After expanding their facility in 2007, they've decided that's it: Dan stated that "we do not have any plans for further expansion beyond continuous improvement projects for energy conservation and beer quality. Absolutely no plans to expand our market. We want to stay small." The husband-wife team is united in its determination to stay local. Deb admits that some think it's odd they're opposed to expansion, but what "I think is weirder is that we're one of the only ones limiting ourselves to one state. It's true that if

I were to sign one of these offers from distributors to reach other states it would be a huge amount of cash for the brewery because it would mean huge orders, but I don't think that's true, meaningful growth. I'm trying to build a business that's going to be around long after I'm gone."

The Careys share a commitment to both their product and their state, a commitment that has shaped both the beer they offer and how they offer it. They turned what might be a disadvantage—a small brewery up against the bigs—into an advantage, garnering national awards and a cultlike following for their brews. Instead of going head-to-head with the dominant players or even mimicking more established craft breweries, they simply went their own way, subverting the "usual" route to success of aggressive marketing followed by rapid expansion. They kept on with their agenda of creating good beers their neighbors would like, and even as their reputation and their company grew, they've maintained that focus. As Dan noted, "We're not interested in being a big brewery. The idea that bigger is better is not necessarily true. Our idea is to be successful in our own backyard."

Like Your Life Depended on It

Young men were dying, and no one knew why. It was the early 1980s, and strange symptoms and diseases were felling men from New York to San Francisco; because these men were gay—at the time, a despised group—few political leaders felt any urgency as the death toll mounted. Dedicated doctors and scientists did eventually pinpoint a cause, HIV, and named the constellation of symptoms AIDS. But while there was a cause and a name, there was no cure: to be infected with HIV meant death from AIDS.

Fear rumbled through the gay community, a fear that turned into anger. While politicians studiously avoided the topic or, even worse, suggested those with HIV be branded or imprisoned, men (and women) continued to die. Playwright Larry Kramer, frustrated with what he saw as a weak response to the crisis, founded ACT UP, whose slogan "Silence = Death" became the mantra of the those determined to push through official apathy and to put a cure for AIDS at the top of the political and scientific agenda. As David France, director of the Oscar-nominated film *How to Survive a Plague*, noted, activists felt: "This government is not paying attention to us. The health establishment is ignoring us. The pharmaceutical industry is not involved in any aspect of research that would do anything to save our lives. Six years into the epidemic, not a single pill available; we've got to do something." ACT UP became known for its noisy protests and outrageous stunts—it shut down the Food and Drug Administration for a day, and over a hundred protesters were arrested after disrupting mass at St. Patrick's Cathedral in New York City; the organization was controversial even in the gay community.

But ACT UP was not just noisy. After a retired organic chemist, Iris Long, happened upon an ACT UP meeting, she argued that protests were not enough: the members of the group had to learn the science and push for research. She had concerns about AZT, the only drug available at the time; at an early meeting, she wrote out her concerns and made a presentation. The others, France reported, "essentially accepted it and put it on their agenda. That was it. It was on the agenda."

As France recounted, "She armed the activists with a goal, which was to transform science and health care in America, and with the language to begin to understand how to do that, and set them railing on a path of this remarkable self-education mission to learn . . . to the point where they literally became a group of self-educated scientists in a way capable of interacting in an effective way, in a productive way, with Nobel Prize winners and people who are really at the benches trying to identify new agents to study and to try to get them into human bodies to see if they would do any good at all."

Mark Harrington, who was among those who formed the Treatment and Data group, one of the many subcommittees to tackle the science of HIV and AIDS, noted that Long and Jim Eigo (another T&D member) had prepared presentations for ACT UP, but these "seemed very academic and they were very full of words that maybe not everybody would immediately understand what they were talking about." The message had to be clear—to both the protesters and their audience. "In those days, a lot of people thought that the FDA actually tested the drugs. They didn't understand that they actually just oversee the testing, which is done by NIH or by industry. So, there was a whole lot of explaining about an institution, a set of regulations and laws, and some scientific concepts that had to be done in two months, so that everybody in ACT UP could understand it, so that we could get across the message to the American people."

The activists did raise the profile of HIV/AIDS, and sympathy rose for those with the disease. Still, it wasn't enough: research was moving slowly, and those infected had difficulty even finding out who was running drug trials, much less getting into them. Harrington credits Long with wiping away the opacity around these trials. "Iris, actually, out of the Treatment and Data Committee, they formed the AIDS Treatment Registry, which became kind of a national model, and it developed a directory of all the studies that were available in New York City and later, in New York State, for people with HIV." ACT UP also pushed the NIH and FDA to revise their recommendations for what few drugs were available. "We wrote to Tony Fauci at NIH and to FDA and Gina Kolata covered it on Page One of the *New York Times* and they changed the dose, they lowered the dose. That was one of the really good things that we did right away."

Others pushed for faster approval for drugs, as well as for opening up promising drugs for compassionate use prior to approval. Peter Staley, who was often the face of demonstrations against the

FDA, noted that "the FDA was born from the scandal of a drug that led to thousands of deformed babies and it was, the entire organization was set up to prevent that type of harm happening again. Quick approval had nothing to do with what it was about. . . . They were just like a stone wall." Sometimes Staley—literally—breached that wall, but at other times he entered through the front door and met with FDA officials. "We had this level of desperation that permitted us to try any and all techniques at the same time. And that ultimately came down to this inside versus outside approach—talking versus civil disobedience, and it had to be one or the other, which I thought was ridiculous." As ACT UP alternately confronted and engaged with the FDA, the stone wall began to give, so much that these efforts didn't just help those with HIV/AIDS: the practice of allowing compassionate use of drugs and the push for faster approval have since been expanded to treatments for other diseases.

Iris Long, reflecting on her involvement with ACT UP, concluded that "anyone can make a difference. And, that you really have to seek and listen to many voices. If my voice wasn't heard— and you have to really do a lot of research, a lot of research in finding out things—trying to figure out why this works this way, and why it doesn't work this way. What are the different pieces to make something work? You have to reach out to all different types of people—whether they're doctors, different communities, churches, whatever. To get things done, you have to make a chart of where you have to go. So, there has to be some sort of a plan, too. You have to plan."

You have to have a plan. The plan of ACT UP was, for many members, quite literally to save their own lives by calling attention to the suffering and death caused by AIDS and alternately shaming and challenging governmental and pharmaceutical company officials to do more. Extreme examples maybe—keep in mind, this was an emergency situation—but amid all the rancor and outrageous acts, the members were also quite practical. They didn't know enough about who and what they were up against, so they had to learn to speak the same language of those who were considered their adversaries. As they educated themselves on the science and research and as they learned about how the bureaucracy functioned, those adversaries were turned into allies. The people in ACT UP were willing to confront, but they were also willing to cooperate. As Peter Staley observed, "It was that combination that I thought was our power, the entire time."

Overcoming Opposition

Innovation and change always meet opposition. Even if no one's paying attention when you begin implementing your agenda, once you start to challenge the "way things are," you will run into headwinds. Determination is absolutely necessary if you're to prevail, but on top of passion and purpose, you need to arm yourself with tactics designed specifically to overcome detractors and break through to those who will support you.

Let's look at the various forms of resistance to innovative agendas:

1. *You're weird.* Jane Addams was met with bewilderment and bemusement from her peers. *Why on earth would anyone want to give up status and reputation to do something so odd and disreputable?* Similarly, fellow brewers shake their heads at the Careys' insistence on limiting their markets to their home state. *You could be big and you choose to remain small?!* In both cases the innovators shook off the naysayers, choosing to make salient and commit to their own agendas rather than submit themselves to standard operating procedures.

   They reinforced this commitment in two ways: One, they saw what they did as common sense. As much as they may have been innovators, they focused on the practical benefits of their plans. As Deb Carey said, what is weird to her is that others *don't* do what New Glarus Brewing does. Two, Addams and the Careys practiced what they preached; they walked the talk. Addams moved into Hull House, showing in her daily living that the gap between rich and poor could be bridged; while the Careys, in focusing on turning out a quality product appreciated by their neighbors, have become profitable without becoming big. Both Addams and the Careys demonstrated that their methods can and do work, making it difficult for others to argue with their success. In the end, others got in on their agenda.

2. *You're trouble.* Luther was condemned as a heretic and ACT UP as subversive. Luther and ACT UP, acting on what they saw as fundamental truths, embraced the role of troublemaker, using it both to draw out opponents and to draw supporters to their sides. They provoked reactions from adversaries they saw as intractable and in so doing made themselves visible as actors capable of sparking change. The very process of catapulting themselves onto the radar allowed them to unfurl their banners above the crowd, to point to the flaws among the powers that be, and to say "Do something!" Once they decided to confront the dominant authorities, they went all out, struggling to make their issues salient, boldly refusing to bend even in the face of arrests and death threats. Whether or not Luther actually said "Here I stand. . . . I can do no other," that cry has resounded through the centuries, steeling dissenters against doubt and dismay.

What also kept them on the path was the cultivation of powerful allies. Luther could count on the support of Frederick the Wise, while ACT UP insinuated itself into the scientific community by learning the science. Those who had been skeptical of the ACT UP members, seeing them as mere rabble-rousers, ended up working with them toward the shared goal of eradicating a dread disease. That Luther and ACT UP both struck out alone did not mean they remained loners; in fact, neither would have succeeded without adding followers and gaining support in unexpected places. While Luther did, in some sense, fail insofar as he was unable to remake the Catholic Church, he did ultimately lead the way to the reformation of Christianity as a whole. ACT UP, which was less interested in reforming the FDA than in saving lives, through its collaboration with the FDA ended up doing both.

Being branded a heretic or troublemaker within your company or field won't mean the loss of your life, but it could mean the loss of your job or promotion opportunities. Seek out sympathetic protectors, and educate yourself on the ways of your skeptics. If your colleagues are satisfied with current procedures and if what you're proposing means big changes in those procedures, they might simply dismiss you as ignorant. Gain a deep understanding of their process, however, and they'll be more willing to listen to your ideas.

3. *Who cares?* Whitaker took AMP overseas at a time when other manufacturers concentrated on the domestic market. It made no sense: the United States was booming, while the postwar economies of Europe and Japan were struggling to recover, so why bother—after all, if it were a good idea to go global, wouldn't someone have already done it?

Whitaker was undeterred, worried less about the apathy of others than the opportunities he calculated he could make for himself. Given that his chances of breaking through the automotive market in the United States were nil, why not take the chance? Raising the issue of going global was an eminently practical decision, and if other companies hadn't thought of it before, well, so much the worse for them. By plunging into markets others were ignoring, Whitaker was able to build his business and make a name for AMP in the rest of the world. By the time others caught on, AMP had already established itself as a truly international enterprise and demonstrated that it was not just possible to work internationally; it was good business.

Addams, too, fought against apathy, albeit of a different sort. Why should anyone bother—"the poor ye shall always have with you" and all that—and why in particular should the privileged care? She built her agenda on the simple premise that every human being has dignity, and she made salient the idea that all people deserve a chance to improve their lot in life. In her day-to-day activities, she showed how the practical application of her ideas could have an effect, which in turn led others to agree that change was possible. And ACT UP, while far more outrageous than the respectable Addams, also broke through the apathy surrounding the suffering of a marginalized group, putting faces and names on what had been anonymous lists of the dead. We are all human, Addams and ACT UP insisted, a basic message that today seems the very essence of common sense.

In all these cases, these agenda setters shredded the veil of ignorance and apathy around their goals by taking concrete steps to achieve their goals. It is easy to get carried away in your own rhetoric or get caught up in high-flying ideas, but as important as those ideals are, you have to be able to bring them down to earth. You can't *force* people to pay attention, but you can make yourself and your plans difficult to ignore.

You are on the radar (or in the door, if you prefer), and you have established (or contributed to) the agenda or subjects to be discussed. Now, in the next chapter, it's time to inject the meaning and angle that will help to bring about the results you want.

Step Three

CHAPTER 8

The Elusive Art of Meaning Making

The *New Yorker* magazine has entertained readers for decades with its smart and funny cartoons. A back-of-the-magazine feature called "Cartoon Caption Contest" offers a new cartoon in every issue, sans caption, that invites readers to submit their own ideas for one. Thousands of submissions pour in each week. Three finalists are announced in a subsequent issue, and a winner, as well as second and third place contestants, is eventually named.

Of interest for us to the process of creating meaning—as well as salience and agenda, incidentally—is that those who submit their 250-character caption in the hopes of seeing their name immortalized in the *New Yorker* have nothing to go on but a few observable concepts in the form of a drawing in a box. In one recent contest, we see a large rat sitting comfortably in a chair reading a newspaper as a middle-aged couple in sleepwear is looking on—the wife holding a phone receiver while appearing to be mouthing something to her husband. So what's going on? Is the rat an oversized pet? An intruder? Why is it holding a newspaper? What is the wife's intent with the phone? Whom might she be calling? What's the husband's stance? Are they even husband and wife? We can speculate, and readers happily do, in the many thousands.

The short answer is that *nothing* is going on until we, the reader, first establish an agenda, a topic for the scene. We get to put words into the mouths of the characters—create salience. And then we get to slant the meaning of those words to elicit a certain understanding for the audience. If we could see the thousands of entries sent in by *New Yorker* readers, we'd see likely as many different scenarios of what the situation means.

In the example of the newspaper-holding rat, the winning caption was "We're gonna need a bigger cat." But it could also have been one of the others, as illustrated in the other two finalists' submissions:

Second place: "He's been on that same story for hours. I'm beginning to think he can't read."

Third place: "Did you just order a hundred cheese pizzas?"

Each caption changes the agenda and the meaning, given only the directly observable "facts" (a few black lines that trigger certain existing mental constructs) of a concerned couple in pajamas and a smug-looking, newspaper-holding, oversized rodent in what looks like a tense situation—but there I go adding meaning already.

By now, in our breakthrough communication process, you'd have, to the best of your ability, engaged in a thoughtful first and second step. Your best, conscientious efforts at getting on someone else's radar and establishing an agenda item have met with success. Time then to reap some of the benefits of your hard work and take the breakthrough communication process to its next level: focusing the meaning of your agenda items for an audience and facilitating the audience's acceptance of that meaning. This is the critical piece that so often leads to desired action on the part of our communication targets—or, if not properly and fully completed, becomes the reason why we lose out on our desired goal. Communication scholar Richard Vatz notes that this is the part of the persuasion process that endows the salience-agenda items with meaning or spin. After you've credibly entered people's awareness and established a list of items they (implicitly or explicitly) agree to focus on, it's time to make it meaningful for them.

The meaning, or spin, step involves infusing deep meaning and resonance in the items of "fact" that you and your audience have thus far agreed are important. Harvard professor Howard Gardner has written extensively on the art of influence. In his 2006 book *Changing Minds,* he describes how a relatively obscure and unlikely British politician named Margaret Thatcher rose to the highest elected office in the United Kingdom by successfully developing the salience of her objective: raising Great Britain to the great heights of power and prosperity which it had previously known but from which, according to her agenda items, it had been allowed to ignominiously fall (in the hands of inept liberal Labour leadership). Thatcher succeeded in part, Gardner persuasively argues, by crafting her set of objectives into a colorful, compelling narrative—a story with which many voting Britons could identify. "Thatcher was able to tap her constituents' sense that their country's greatness had been marginalized," writes Gardner. Thus, her objectives, strengthening the military and weakening the welfare state among others, which had not been valued by a prior generation of voters, were now knit together in a compelling story—if only it could be achieved. Soon after her election, Prime Minister Thatcher successfully prosecuted a war against Argentina over a cluster of relatively unimportant islands, the Falklands (or Las Malvinas to the Argentines), which permitted her meaning to play out in very real life (and death) terms.

Engendering meaning (or spin) allows you to focus your objective and guide your communication toward what is really your sought-after outcome. Let's say you are the CEO of a major consumer goods corporation. Tough times have made it necessary for you to lay off several hundred, or thousand, employees. Your target is a journalist or perhaps the news media in general. Because of your position, you are already on the radar. Because you have decided to proactively communicate to the media that your concern is about announcing layoffs, you have set the agenda, provided the media buy in.

So far, these two steps (in this scenario) have not constituted a challenge in and of themselves. Here is the hard part: How do you position and define your statement of layoffs such that you are not judged (to the best of your ability) greedy, thoughtless, or detached from the concerns of the everyday folk who make up your employee and customer base? Now, it's true that journalists will tell the story they want to tell, even doggedly propagating a counterstory (remember, you are always competing with others' agendas in the struggle to make individual issues salient). But you have to be active in creating the meaning you feel will lead to a most favorable outcome: considering the layoffs to be wise or, at the very least, getting "your side of the story" some coverage in the public discussion. In this interest, the CEO can communicate something along the lines of, "We regret that layoffs have to occur. But rather than looking at this as an arbitrary decision, we want to convey that (1) we first made every possible, feasible, nonpersonnel cut before coming to this decision, (2) we believe that it is absolutely necessary to take these steps in order to ensure the long-term survivability of our company, (3) cutting positions [*note*: not 'cutting people'] will allow us to ride out this storm that has hit all levels of the national economy, thus putting us in a good position to rehire and create more jobs down the line, and (4) we continue to urge our national policy makers to introduce legislation that will facilitate business conditions in this country and thus make it much less likely that we will need to eliminate workforce positions." While the people in the media business may not believe or agree with the counterstory being put forth, it at least gives them something to consider. It is hoped, too, they will at least convey these ideas to a national argument by way of objective reporting—though in these kinds of cases you shouldn't hold your breath. Boiled down to its root elements, the CEO is taking the agenda item of layoffs and giving it the following meaning: We are not heartless; we didn't want to do this. By doing this, we are enabling ourselves to rehire later on. And government bears some of the blame for our plight.

In the wake of the horrific school shooting massacre in Newtown, Connecticut, an agenda item became instantly burned—or reburned—onto the national political radar. I am, of course, talking about gun control. This was a case of what Vatz calls exigency: something big happens in reality and as a result is then emblazoned on our minds. (Of course, the fact that President

Obama chose specifically to pursue gun control as a political item shows how he actively put it on the national agenda as well.) Barely a week after that terrible day in December 2012, when victims' funerals and memorial services were literally still happening, the wrangling over meaning began to dominate the media. It was the usual tussle: people in favor of gun control saw in the Newtown narrative a link between gun deregulation and murdered children. An advertisement by the NRA, which showed President Obama's daughters receiving taxpayer-funded Secret Service security, tried to link gun control to elitism, paternalism, and liberalism.

Amid all this hue and cry, however, a Washington, D.C., attorney and mother of six named Gayle Trotter took the agenda item of gun control and infused it with yet another meaning. It would be easy to assume that any mother might identify with the parents of the Newtown children. Not Trotter. Instead, she called efforts to delimit gun ownership sexist and antifeminist. Why? Because in her view, guns empowered women. "An assault weapon in the hands of a young woman defending her babies in her home becomes a defense weapon," said Trotter in testimony, as reported by the *Huffington Post*. Whether you agree with Gayle Trotter's tack or not, it is noteworthy; she came up with a distinctive and unusual spin on a predictable, if heated and high-stakes, political controversy. When you are seeking to construct meaning, think of what the current, well-known arguments are—and then see if you can find a new angle.

There are other examples of meaning makers who seek to put a fresh spin on agenda items, sometimes making the humdrum into the controversial. Marissa Mayer, CEO of Yahoo! recently—and inadvertently I might add—turned flextime and work-from-home policies into something of a political crucible. As many might know, Mayer, a numbers-driven executive, looked at statistics that indicated to her that employees who worked from home were, as a group, less productive. She thus ordered all Yahoo! employees to work in their brick-and-mortar office space. Pundits, complainers, dissatisfied workers, and observers, however, infused the agenda item—work-from-home privileges—with sociopolitical meaning. It was suggested, for example, that Mayer's policy was tinged with sexism and classism. "The argument goes that either Mayer should support her 'own kind' or that she is not a 'real' working mother because she is a wealthy CEO who has built her own nursery next to her office," wrote *Forbes* online.

I believe that all steps in our breakthrough communication process are of equal importance, and so far in this book, we've seen how to get noticed (or get on the radar) and how to bring up your aims (by adding them to an agenda). But I feel equally strong that the step we're discussing here: infusing your agenda item with meaning, is probably the most challenging and critical to the entire process.

To Spin or Not to Spin

If you were a journalist turned cable pundit who was contributing to the myriad daily left- or right-wing news sources or other political-leaning cable channels out there, you'd have shed your "reporter" hat in favor of the one reading "op-ed contributor." There are facts, and then there is the way in which those facts are conveyed so as to make someone else think or feel a certain way. We intuitively know this holds for us too in our everyday life.

Let's say your product is selling better with an 18–35 demographic than it used to. These are numbers, data, facts. But when you suggest that it all means your product has a "youthful" or "edgy" appeal, you are giving those changed statistics *meaning*; you are asking someone to look at them and think and feel differently, because there is a *viable or compelling interpretation* of those facts. We call it making meaning, and it's an essential part of the four-step process of breakthrough communication. Making meaning is the step that forms, clarifies, and sharpens your communication effort because it puts it in the realm of understanding and emotion.

Former U.K. prime minister Margaret Thatcher was masterful at this. As I alluded to earlier in this chapter, in 1982, the Falkland Islands, a British territory off the coast of South America, were invaded by Argentina. That much was a fact. In a sense, the Argentine military put the Falklands—a collection of islands some 310 miles from the South American mainland—on the radar. Ms. Thatcher wanted to take military action against the Argentines. She gained popular support to do so by making such action part of a larger narrative about Britain recovering its fading glory and proving its strength at a time of both perceived and actual decline. Another leader, one who wanted to avoid a larger conflict, might have spun the story as, say, searching for a peaceful compromise or letting go of a meaningless patch of territory. But the Prime Minister made meaning—and in so doing, marshaled public support for her war—by putting the Argentine aggression and her proposed counterattack within the narrative of history. Two months and twelve days after they had invaded, the Argentine forces surrendered.

Another great example of masterful meaning making comes also from military history by way of that greatest of storytellers, William Shakespeare. The Bard wrote a series of dramas sometimes called the Henry cycle because they deal with the story of King Henry IV and King Henry V over the course of four different plays. While the plot of these plays revolves around the consolidation of power in the kingdom of England, from various battles between dueling royals to King Henry V's glorious conquest of France, it also tells the tale of a young Prince Harry maturing into adulthood.

In his youth, Harry was a brigand, a drunk, a playboy, and a vandal. He hung out with his pals, including corpulent boozehound

Sir John Falstaff, whose friendship he cherished (and vice versa) but whose influence made him ill suited to rise to the office of king. Had *People* and *Us* magazines been around back then, they would have loved it! When it comes time to assume the robes of royalty, however, Prince Harry, now King Henry V, knows he has to, ever so painfully, give the heave-ho to his former drinking buddies, Falstaff and the lot of them. It's like the mailroom clerk who knows he's going to be CEO someday because his family owns the company. It's one thing to get smashed and carry on at the office Christmas party, however embarrassing. But when you're in charge of the whole thing, it's an entirely different matter; things have to change. The former Prince Harry, now King Henry, knows this in his gut. When the ambassador from France visits Henry bearing insults and threats from the French crown prince, the Dauphin, the young English king tells the envoy that "we understand him well, How he comes o'er us with our wilder days." But, he adds, "tell the Dauphin I will keep my state, Be like a king, and show my sail of greatness." In other words, Henry knows he was a major screwup as a prince. But that's all over now. He's king; he's different. And he wants his enemies to take note.

Having rallied his subjects, proven his virtue, and gathered supporters to achieve his main desire—the conquest of France—King Henry finds himself near the field of Agincourt in France, ready to meet the opposing army. There is just one problem: he is vastly outnumbered. His troops have been warring for months in a foreign land. They are undersupplied, hungry, and ragged. What's more, their morale is starting to falter. The French, on the other hand, have many thousands of soldiers. They are well fed and flush with munitions, and they are properly rested and fighting on their home turf, unimpeded by a channel of water between them and their headquarters of operations. It's as if Henry is getting ready to roll out his big, new product, and his employees are simply on the verge of giving up. It's not that they don't care. It's that the odds are steeply against them, and frankly, they don't want to get slaughtered. Henry, however, by way of Shakespeare, is a brilliant meaning maker. (Again, he also knows how to spark action, as we will see, but it's his use of narrative that we want to underscore here.)

It is midfall in the year 1415. Morning. King Henry looks out over his ragtag army, and even *he* is not sure if he and his soldiers can pull this one off. The mighty bluster of the French army can be heard not far off. Many of Henry's soldiers taste cold fear in their throats. Henry's own cousin, and one of his commanders, Westmoreland, remarks, "O that we now had here But one ten thousand of those men in England That do no work today!" It's a logical wish. A few more guys. Just to even the odds. And here is King Henry's brilliance, the moment when he takes just that fear, just that quite plausible wish, and turns it around into the fiery meaning that will ultimately steel his troops and make them follow him gloriously and unflinchingly into battle against the kingdom of France.

No, says Henry, no more men. We have enough. "If we are marked to die, we are enough To do our country loss; and if to live, The fewer men, the greater share of honor." That's the *meaning* that Henry has injected into his current action: he is not asking his troops merely to pick a fight with a much bigger enemy. No. He is offering all present the chance to *become legends,* to leave the day, dead or alive, sheathed in honor. "I am not covetous for gold," Henry tells his assembled army, "But if it be a sin to covet honor, I am the most offending soul alive." No, he tells Westmoreland (and all else who may be similarly inclined), "wish not a man from England." In fact, the inspiring young king goes on to say, if anyone wants to leave, despite the numerical odds, he'll gladly let him go. In fact, he'll pay for the trip, "crowns for convoy put into his purse"! Because what remains will be a feast of honor, all the more honor to go around for those who stay and fight.

Ever the brilliant tactician and rhetorician, Henry notices that today is the Feast of St. Crispian (actually two Christian martyrs from the third century, Crispin and Crispinian). Yet he tells the members of his military throng, it will henceforth be the day when the tale of *their* greatness at the Battle of Agincourt, the brave and glorious British against the vastly better-equipped French, is celebrated by all. "He that shall live this day, and see old age, Will yearly on the vigil feast his neighbors And say, 'Tomorrow is Saint Crispian.' Then will he strip his sleeve and show his scars, And say 'These wounds I had on Crispin's day.'" Those who partook will become legends. "Then shall our names, Familiar in his mouth as household words—Harry the King, Bedford and Exeter, Warwick and Talbot, Salisbury and Gloucester—Be in their flowing cups freshly remember'd. This story shall the good man teach his son; And Crispin Crispian shall ne'er go by, From this day to the ending of the world, But we in it shall be remember'd."

Did it have the effect Henry was looking for? Westmoreland, who just a few minutes earlier was wishing for a boatload of recruits from home, now tells his lord and master, "God's will, my liege! Would you and I alone, Without more help, could fight this royal battle." That's some powerful meaning making. Not only has Henry turned the doubting Westmoreland around 180 degrees—and, presumably, any other nervous Nellies in his ranks—but he has made it seem an unhappy curse *not* to be there, ranged against a huge army to whom they are almost sure to lose. Of course, if Henry is a brilliant tactician and arguer, ultimately, he is so in this scene because the play's author, William Shakespeare, understood what motivated others to act in one's interest even in times of terrible adversity. Rather than saying, "Look, I know we're outnumbered, but here we are, and you're my subjects, and you promised to fight, and maybe, who knows, it won't go so badly after all, and if it does, well, we can just run away . . . ," and so forth, Shakespeare's King Henry makes meaning *of the very adversity* that threatens to rob his endeavor of meaning—the adversity of near-certain decimation.

Many times, a communicator is responding to adversity or the possibility thereof. An organization, a work group, a team, a project faces some kind of seemingly impossible challenge. It's not enough to simply say, "Somehow we'll get it done!" Of course, the undertaking must be carefully considered and reappraised. Henry himself is quite canny and aware of the chances he has chosen to take, sometimes sounding more cautious in private than before his assembled followers. But especially in the face of adversity, knowing how to get others to follow your plan may mean tying the current threat into the larger story unfolding. You are not down and defeated; you are *learning from past mistakes* or *returning to former greatness.*

Henry, of course—at least in Shakespeare's retelling—rouses his troops so effectively with the meaning of St. Crispian's Day that they rout the French with ridiculous ferocity. "The day is yours," concedes a defeated French battlefield emissary to the British sovereign. In Shakespeare's version, no doubt making things that much more dramatic, somehow the French have lost 10,000 troops, while the English have lost 30. Such a miracle was only to be undone, in time, by another influential meaning maker, a young French girl named Joan who heard voices. But that is another story for another time.

It may take someone with a creative vision to weave meaning into events, but it's crucial to do so. In fact, the bigger the bogey-man one is facing, the more important it is to find a meaning with resonance, the kind of thing that will turn an agenda item into something truly worth fighting for. I suspect that a number of tech innovators—even some destined to become household names—motivate themselves and others by casting their efforts in the classic David-taking-on-Goliath narrative, the outgunned but smart and nimble guys and gals in a garage working on the next big thing, so big in fact that it will take the giant names in Silicon Valley and on Wall Street by glorious surprise. In business, education, the arts, government, healthcare, and our own day-to-day lives, there are always chances for subtle, well-placed St. Crispian's Day speeches of our own.

Now—while we're at it—let's recall another famous moment from Shakespeare that is also an epic case of spin and framing of an issue. In *Julius Caesar*, the title character has been struck down by a group of conspirators who felt that he was just too powerful and posed a threat to Roman democracy. Once they've done that, they have to decide fast whether to also kill Caesar's loyal friend and second-in-command, Mark Antony, who they think is not going to be on their side. One of the main conspirators, Brutus, essentially says to the others: hey—don't worry about Antony, what can he do? In fact, Brutus says, we'll let Antony give a eulogy at Caesar's funeral like he wants to, just so everyone will know that we're not tyrants ourselves, that we believe in freedom of speech, and that there are no hard feelings. And don't worry about whatever Antony might say, because I'll speak first and explain the situation to everyone. What could go wrong?

So Brutus gets up at the big public funeral and says, basically: Okay, be quiet everybody. I'm here to tell you that we had really good reasons for killing Caesar. If you think you were better off with Caesar alive, then you're either a fool or a coward for choosing to be no more than slaves. We've written down all our reasons in a manifesto, and you can go look them up. Then he introduces Antony. At this point the crowd is pretty much accepting Brutus.

So what does Antony do? First, he thanks Brutus graciously for allowing him to speak. Then he says you know, Caesar was my friend, so maybe I'm not one to judge right and wrong here. I'm not one to argue with what Brutus says; maybe Caesar really was like he says, even if we only knew him as a soldier and fearless leader and a friend. Then Antony chokes up.

After a second, in which the people start muttering sympatheti-cally for him, he goes on: Thanks again to Brutus and the guys for letting me speak, and I'm definitely not going to let myself say any-thing that would give you reasons to be mad at them. Have you heard that Caesar left all his money to you, the people of Rome, in his will? Oh you didn't know that?

I'm sorry. I don't think I was supposed to say that. Forget it. I wasn't supposed to say that. Never mind that; let's just look at Julius Caesar. I just recognized this shirt he's wearing—I was with him when he got it. Now it's all hacked up. You can actually see right here the first knife cut from where Cassius stabbed him. And I think *this* one is from Cassius. And this one here . . . that's Brutus. You *know* that one hurt, considering Caesar loved Brutus like a son, and what must it have been like for him to realize in his last seconds who was going to be his killer. To be honest, I think Caesar just died of a broken heart right then. Now, don't you cry about it. I didn't mean to make you upset about this. We all know these are honorable gentlemen, so whatever personal beef they had with Caesar, I'm sure they felt they were right, and maybe they were. Look, I'm not trying to start any trouble here or play politics with this. I'm not a great speaker like Brutus. I'm just tak-ing a moment to remember my good friend.

By the time Antony finished speaking, the crowd was whipped into a rage about the killing, and Brutus and his friends barely escaped from the city with their lives. Why is Antony able to motivate the crowd in the way he wants? It all comes back to the things that we have been talking about in this book. By being Caesar's right-hand man, of course, Antony was already "on the radar" in Roman society. But he was getting on the radar in another sense, getting airtime if you will, when he asked Brutus if he could speak at the funeral. In order to do that, he had to first establish "common ground" with Brutus's gang, which he does in a famous scene just after the murder, by shaking all the killers' bloody hands and making them think he is willing to see things from their point of view. Once he gets into the funeral pulpit, though, he immediately begins *setting the agenda,* even though he does it in a gradual and stealthy way. That agenda, of course, is to turn the tables on the assassins, and he succeeds by aggressively reframing the political debate.

If Henry the Fifth's speech at Agincourt is a great example of spin and rhetorical framing, Antony's funeral speech is a study in how one particular spin on an event, Caesar's assassination (i.e., "It was the murder of a great man"), can be unleashed to combat someone else's spin on the same event ("It was the liberation of Rome from tyranny"). Framing, as we've seen, is a matter of establishing exactly what we should be talking about at a given moment and by the same token what we should be ignoring. From the conspirators' point of view, we should be talking about the principle of freedom and ignoring the pain and suffering of Julius Caesar as he died, as well as ignoring the virtues that he had when he was alive. From Antony's point of view, it is the opposite: We should be talking about both Caesar's greatness as a Roman leader and his goodness as a friend, both of which will make his killing seem like a shocking crime. And we should be ignoring, from Antony's point of view, the whole abstract political philosophy that was the conspirators' justification. Same facts, different meaning. Caesar is dead. Does his death mean the liberation of Rome, or is its meaning just that of a brutal act of violence by men who should never have been trusted?

You might think that the liberating of a country would be the stronger one of the two interpretations, because it is such a hugely large-scale matter in comparison with the death of one man. But, in fact, the opposite is true psychologically: because we think of everything fundamentally in terms of human experience, the story of a man being murdered by his friend actually carries more direct impact for us than the description of a big development in politics. So it seems that Antony had a stronger hand to play, a better story to tell.

But he didn't just hold better cards; he played them better too. Brutus, remember, starts by telling people *to be quiet*; he talks down to them; he appeals more to cognitive meaning than emotional meaning. He pretty much has a tin ear. But Antony couldn't be more different. He seems gracious and humble. He thanks Brutus for *allowing* him to speak, which is nice on the surface but also emphasizes that Brutus has become pretty high and mighty if he's suddenly saying who can speak and who can't. Antony uses a direct emotional appeal: "He was my friend . . . ," he says. And later he notes, "When that the poor have cried, Caesar hath wept," and he gets choked up.

We've talked about self-examination to access the right motives. Antony does this; he is not just pretending to be angry about the murder of his friend, when he finally tips his hand in the speech and makes it clear that this is his real attitude. He also uses narrative to reach his audience: "I remember the first time ever Caesar put [the garment] on; 'Twas on a summer evening in his tent, the day he overcame the Nervii . . ." He doesn't boss his listeners or insist on how they should view the situation. He coaxes them by giving them a chance to realize his viewpoint and emotion *as their own emotion*. Antony's speech, in short, is classic breakthrough communication: he is tapping deeply into the present moment and sparking action in a group of people.

It is amazing to think about the fact that whatever the precise wording that Shakespeare's imagination supplied for Henry the Fifth and for Mark Antony—and precise wording is important, as we'll discuss in the next chapter—these instances of breakthrough communication really happened in some form, and they had real-world consequences. Henry really did motivate his troops somehow at Agincourt, and Antony really did sway the Roman public against Caesar's assassins, and both of them changed the course of world history.

Of course, as I've been suggesting throughout *Breakthrough Communication*, you don't need to be a CEO or prominent general—a Marissa Mayer, Margaret Thatcher, Henry the Fifth, or Mark Antony—to take an idea, put it on the agenda, and infuse it with novel meaning; you just have to have a clear understanding of the realities of communication and a determination to put them into practice in order to achieve what you want to achieve.

In the next chapter we'll take a closer look at how meaning is created with specific language and the myriad of words at our disposal.

CHAPTER 9

How Language Creates Meaning

f you've ever sold a "preowned" vehicle, complained about "those bureaucrats in Washington," or "downsized" a business unit, you've engaged in more than just selling a used car, voicing your concern about government officials, or firing people at work; you've engaged in creating meaning with language, to some desired end. Language—we dress it up when it suits us, saying "preowned" for *used*; we dress it down when sharing our frustration, calling politicians "bureaucrats"; and we address it carefully when we refer to the termination or firing of people as "downsizing." In virtually every aspect of our lives, we can observe how meaning creation is accomplished with the use of selective wording, framing, and spin, most noticeable perhaps in advertising, politics, media coverage, and the arts.

As Chip Souba, MD, has written, "Language itself . . . is constitutive of the realities of our experience, opening up to us a uniquely *human* world. Language is the bridge between the created present and the uncreated future." Everyone knows language can have great impact on the outcome of a person-to-person exchange, but how often do we actually stop to think about exactly how this works? What do I need to pay attention to if I want to make that bridge to the future or get that desired outcome—that customer to buy my product, that client to sign a contract, that voter to vote for me, or even that potential romantic partner to agree to go on a date?

The Impact of Language

In breakthrough communication, we use language strategically to manage meaning. One such strategy revolves around the concepts of precision and vagueness. To be sure, all too often we get this wrong. We're vague when we should be precise and precise when we should communicate in more vague terms. For instance, we might advise a subordinate to work on his communication skills—a vague and not very helpful suggestion for lack of specificity—when the chap's offending issue really is, say, a tendency to be too verbose in meetings, coupled with a habit to interrupt others or speak over them. Precise communication—plain to see—is in order when we are seeking a specific outcome. Whenever we want others to take away our intended meaning beyond a shadow of a doubt, we should be as specific and precise as possible. Asking someone to present the "financials" at an upcoming board meeting may seem specific, but if it's the story behind a precipitous slide in margins you're really interested in, you may only get a superficial treatment on the topic you're most after, having left too much room for interpretation with the more vague, all-numbers-encompassing term *financials*. To get what you want, you would say, "Mary, at tomorrow's meeting, would you please give us a breakdown and some context around the loss of margins in the turbine engine division over the last quarter?"

But are there times and situations when vague communication is in order? The short answer is yes, specifically when we want to let others inject their own meaning into our utterances—when we want to leave interpretation up to them, again, to some strategic end. That "end" could be a number of things, e.g., empowering people to think for themselves, come up with creative solutions instead of simply following instructions, build rapport, or soften the blow at constructive feedback meetings.

For the moment, let's circle back to our executive who asked Mary to present the financials at an upcoming meeting. Depending on the executive's strategic objectives, he might just leave his request vague to see what Mary makes salient at the meeting. Will she downplay the loss of margins? Will she make another issue salient instead? For a strategic communicator, her choices in presenting the financials will be telling.

Vague communication can, as mentioned, serve a multitude of objectives, not the least of which is relationship management. For instance, to avoid putting someone in a group on the spot by saying, "Mark, you haven't said much during this discussion; what are your thoughts regarding the opportunities to streamline fulfillment processes for this proposal?" you might approach the introverts more along the lines of, "We've heard some valuable feedback already; are there other ideas that might add value to the discussion, perhaps in the area of fulfillment?"

There are, of course, many ways to phrase something in more general terms. And if it's collaborative problem solving you'd like to move along at the point of a creative block, it would be better to say, "What are some unconventional, counterintuitive even, ideas—perhaps from other industries—we haven't thought of that might inject some new perspectives into this?" rather than, "I see we're not getting any further with option A; why don't we try option B or C?" Allowing others to inject their own meaning and interpretation can do wonders for relationships and productivity, not to mention creative thinking.

Under the general heading of precision and vagueness, we have a couple of other topics that should be of interest: one of them is the oft-derided "passive voice"—such as the assertion of "mistakes *were made*" instead of "*I made* a mistake." We'd all prefer it if people we deal with took responsibility for their own mistakes. But in the real world, where the *who* might be someone on our own team and a face to the outside world, the active voice may be beside the point and even counterproductive, if what we really want is not necessarily to duck responsibility but rather to convey the idea of *moving on*. And it could be that "mistakes were made" by any number of people, and therefore naming them would make little sense; or perhaps the agent making the mistake is unknown, just like the subject in our passive statement.

So passive voice can be our friend in an outcomes-oriented communication context. "Budget cuts *were deemed* necessary" can equally serve a purpose as "*I decided to* cut the budget," the latter of which can make you look like a no-nonsense leader—at the risk of having the spotlight, or blame, squarely rest on you. The desired perception should be a guide here. I read an example somewhere—the source escapes me—where former U.S. secretary of state Colin Powell responded to an inquiry about reports from the International Committee of the Red Cross about prisoner abuse at Abu Ghraib. To paraphrase his response, "We're looking at those recent reports again to see which ones *we acted on* and which ones *weren't acted on.*" Using both active and passive voice in the same sentence can skew the meaning, however slightly, in one's favor: "we acted on," and away from culpability; "weren't acted on."

Another very good reason to use the passive voice is if the action and the object are far more important to communicate than the subject—the *who*—in the action. As veteran journalist John McIntyre writes on this issue in his blog on language in the *Baltimore Sun*: "The university president was arrested and accused of drunken driving." Who arrested him? Who'd you think arrested him, the faculty senate? You can assume that the police arrested him. The more important information is who got behind the wheel while hammered, and the passive construction allows you to put that information up front in the sentence for more impact."

Yet another case of precision versus vagueness can be found in those humble pronouns *it, this,* and *that.* Legendary New England Patriots coach Bill Belichick is one notable adherent of a simple yet powerful philosophy: "It is what it is"; his favorite saying expresses realism about the world, a level-headed, even-keeled approach with no illusions. It also shows that he has resilience and isn't easily rattled. He has the ability to accept the hand he's been dealt, and he has the ability to say essentially, hey, I'm not going to try to excuse this or explain it away or tell you what you should think about it; you can see what's going on as well as I can. This stance of seemingly leaving room for interpretation is also a crucial part of breakthrough communication. But notice I said "*seemingly* leaving room." The reality is that leaving room for others to interpret meaning and make up their own mind on an issue may, again, create a positive relationship vibe that can lead others gently to your desired perception or outcome.

That said, Belichick's "It is what it is" is worth looking at a bit closer for its effects. The power lies in the "it." Pronouns, like *it,* have a natural role in language as placeholders for particular nouns or groups of nouns. If you use a noun, you specify. And if you use a pronoun in tandem with a noun ("I like New Orleans. *It* feels like home"), then you still specify, just in a more flexible way. But if you use a pronoun *without any noun at all,* the way that Bill Belichick does, then you leave interpretation open. Your meaning isn't limited. It is anyone's ball game—to push the metaphor. Pronouns, therefore, are another way that a little bit of vagueness can help bring about positive outcomes by keeping open the doors of communication that might shut prematurely if one were totally explicit.

Besides precision and vagueness, another important distinction that is of use to the breakthrough communicator is connotation (or what I call "emotive meaning") and denotation (or what I call "cognitive meaning"). Cognitive meaning is the exact, literal, dictionary definition of a word, without any judgment implied about whether it is good or bad, right or wrong.

Emotive meaning, on the other hand, is how a given term makes your listener feel when he or she hears it. Try *torture* versus *enhanced interrogation techniques*. Which one conjures emotions almost immediately? For breakthrough communication, it will pay off to pay close attention to both the cognitive meaning and the emotive meaning of words, with either to be used whenever a certain situation calls for it. You have to know which words will offend or stir your listener and which words will create positive emotions. Names are an example of one kind of word that can be loaded with emotional meanings. There is a reason why only lunatic parents with strong white supremacist leanings would call their newborn "Adolf," while the rest of us recoil in disbelief. Similarly, the mere mention of the aforementioned Abu Ghraib, the more recent (and as of this writing salient) topic of Benghazi, and other names associated with painful emotions can inject strong meaning into any discourse.

Once neutral terms, such as *segregation*, have over time, since the civil rights movement in the United States, cemented a meaning in our collective minds that is almost exclusively negative. Similarly emotive is the term *apartheid* in South Africa. Terms like *affirmative action* too are loaded with emotive meaning. Ask any two people of any gender and race, and the opinions on such a topic will vary as widely as the emotions are strong. In our business world, terms like *restructuring*, the aforementioned *downsizing*, or *mergers and acquisitions* can send shivers of fear through the rank and file, lest it means that one will get the proverbial axe in the process. For executive leaders the words might carry less of a negative weight, as a streamlined organization typically benefits those leading it. The point should be clear: if your objective is to manage relationships and outcomes with others, it makes good sense to be aware of the myriad meanings and connotations language carries with it.

In that last example, you have words that are positive or negative in their emotive meaning depending on the recipient. But many words have become, through their usage over time, basically positively or negatively charged with emotion for pretty much everyone. A word that has built-in positive spin is often called a *euphemism*. Take, for instance, the term *freedom fighter*. When we hear that term, we assume that the person must be fighting in a good cause, one that we would not only agree with but probably be proud to support ourselves. But if we hear the word *insurgent*, we are—through conditioning—likely going to assume the opposite— that the person is fighting for a narrow and rigid ideology, or is even just fighting for the sake of fighting, and we'd most likely not be in favor of his or her actions; that's an example of *dysphemism*, or a word with a negative spin. To put this into context, colonial Americans, fighting against British rule in the 1770s, were likely not referred to as "freedom fighters" but as something more closely resembling today's "insurgents" or "terrorists."

The general idea in meaning making via words is, of course, to use the words that elicit the meaning we want a listener to take away. To do this successfully means having to be dialed in to the zeitgeist and the salient topics of the day in just about any category—from business to politics to entertainment to culture to sports to you name it. By observing the various slants given to certain terminology, we can harness the power of the word for breakthrough communication. In the absence of this knowledge, achieving a careful neutrality in speech and writing, and avoiding any clear-cut cases of euphemism and dysphemism, might—however difficult to achieve—be a safer course of action in people management.

Two more considerations in the effective use of language are credibility and status, both obviously desirable perceptions in the eyes of the proverbial beholders. A straightforward path to a certain amount of credibility can be the mastery of cognitive meaning and vast amounts of knowledge, like a "policy wonk" in

Washington who knows chapter and verse of all the legislation on a subject. GOP congressman and vice presidential candidate Paul Ryan in 2012 was an example of a political figure widely regarded as having tremendous credibility in discussing the federal budget because—agree or disagree with the man—he had (seemingly) done his homework and he knew how to connect the dots for people, which perhaps surprisingly is not something that could be said about every legislator.

A different kind of credibility has been central to the career of Senator John McCain, who saw both combat and imprisonment as a POW during the Vietnam War and therefore could always speak with considerable authority about issues of war and peace as well as veterans' issues; even people who disagree with many of his policy positions on domestic issues have to respect the integrity of the man as far as serving his country and sincerely caring for its veterans.

As far as status is concerned, being a "high-status" participant in any communication can be critical—see the early part of this book, about "getting on the radar." Here too, however, as with the question of vagueness versus precision, sometimes a more round-about or even counterintuitive approach is best. Your status is always relative to other people and to the context in which you are dealing with them, and sometimes the most beneficial strategy for you in the long run is to let *them* have the high status that they need as a condition of working *with* you rather than *against* you. If you diminish people's status through the language you use, the chances of bringing them around to sharing your point of view or your goals may diminish. Then there are times when it's most advantageous to be seen as "high status" yourself and accordingly to use a *powerful* style of speaking—to be decisive, firm, and unapologetic in the way you phrase things.

On the other hand, there are also times when you might want to consider a "medium" or sometimes even a "low" status; you might want to present yourself as simply a colleague, a peer, a servant even, or perhaps a humble and lowly novice, someone who is eager to learn from superiors and who is perceived as respecting their knowledge, their experience, and their views on myriad issues. In these situations you might, paradoxically, gain more influence in the outcomes you seek by adopting a relatively powerless voice: asking and listening, being humble in putting forward assertions of your own that might conflict with theirs.

A relevant phenomenon that academic linguists have studied is that of rhetorical convergence and divergence. Basically, when we want to be accepted by people—and to signal our acceptance of them and their point of view—we tend to adjust our speech so that it more closely resembles theirs. And likewise when we want to show some disagreement with people or a rejection of their ideas, we tend to use speech patterns that contrast starkly with theirs. Considering the established scientific backing of this, it's worth taking note of. Clearly for breakthrough communication, convergence rather than divergence will tend to be the more productive of the two patterns; if you notice you're taking on much of the terminology of a person you are conversing with, it may be a good sign for your prospects of winning him or her around to a meeting of the minds—if, that is, while you are able to yield on the battleground of language, you are holding on firmly to your objective and unique point of view. Of course, the need for a little give-and-take, or a healthy balance, is a given. Shun the temptation to pander too much—without a wink to irony—like stump-speech-giving politicians who clumsily try to put on a down-home, folksy drawl, completely alien to their normal speech, as they campaign in rural areas of the country.

Regularly thinking about our own speech habits in this light can be one valuable form of what I've elsewhere identified as a key principle of breakthrough communication: the self-examination necessary to access the right emotions for effective connection in

141

any given context. Your objective will always be to share meaning with the people in your audience and facilitate their acceptance of that meaning. And to do this you will have to infuse resonance into the issues that you're making salient and that your listeners agree are important. This resonance is fundamentally a matter of emotion. Let's consider some particular cases.

Examples of Breakthrough Communication

One of the most clear-cut areas of successful breakthrough communication—that is, an area where effective communication can be seen to produce quantifiable, tangible results—is the realm of advertising. Every truly successful mass market advertising slogan brings tens of millions of dollars to the company that was shrewd and savvy enough to recognize its strong communicative potential. Without even going into the many dimensions of artistry in advertising—the jingles, the visuals, the full media campaigns—I will point to a few ads that were already winners purely by virtue of their language.

One of these is the timeless slogan "Reach out and touch someone" that was adopted by AT&T. The key thing to notice here is that the slogan has layers of meaning that reinforce each other, even though it is only a few words. To "reach out" to someone usually means to take the initiative both in "getting in touch" with the person and in opening up emotionally. To "touch someone," in everyday speech, generally means to make an impression on the person's heart, to move the person emotionally. So with "reach out," AT&T is inviting you to go out on a limb, take that chance, initiate a human connection. And with "touch someone," the company is offering you the promise that not only will you try, but you will resoundingly succeed. The statement "Reach out and touch someone," taken all together, also conveys a vivid image of being together with another person, in very close, even intimate, proximity, and of making that very personal, bonding gesture of physically touching the person, which we do not ordinarily do unless we are very comfortable with someone. Looked at in this way, the slogan quickly conveys three ideas: emotional openness, success, and togetherness. Because AT&T is a telephone company, obviously, it has every interest in having the consumer firmly associate these three ideas, or ideals, with the notion of doing business with AT&T as opposed to a competitor company. The ad campaign succeeded brilliantly.

"Raise your hand if you're sure," the slogan of Sure brand antiperspirant and deodorant, similarly has a clever layering of meanings: First, raise your hand if you like our product; we're taking a vote or a survey; we care what you think, and we have an easy, informal relationship such that we know you won't hesitate to express your opinion by throwing your hand into the air and being seen and counted. Second, of course, go ahead and show the world your underarm area, which—since you've used our product—is going to be fresh and clean, which it wouldn't be if you hadn't used our product. (Note how in this case the framing of the scene has both a positive side and a negative side, a carrot and a stick, psychologically.) The phrase "if you're sure" can appeal to people's self-image, because they like to feel sure about things, especially when other people maybe aren't so sure, so their own sureness feels like a strength and a virtue. The idea of being sure of yourself and feeling self-confident (as a result of not being ashamed of your sweatiness) is thus somehow merged with the more specific idea that you are so sure of your preference for Sure that you will reach up and be counted for it.

Nike's massively successful slogan "Just do it" is a bit different from the ones already discussed, because it doesn't depend on any kind of pun or double meaning (unless we want to consider the phrase "do it" as carrying a slight sexual association that makes the phrase more forceful and memorable, which is not unheard of in advertising). The main way it works, I think, is by implicitly empowering the people to whom it is addressed—giving them permission to do whatever it is they really want to do deep down, even though something may have been holding them back. It says, I know you are really a doer, a decisive person; go ahead and be that person. Since the ad is, of course, addressed to people who might be thinking about buying shoes and specifically Nikes, it has the added benefit of making that very purchase one of the likely things that people might feel empowered to do when they see or hear the slogan. This slogan resembles both of the last two slogans in the crucial effect it has of empowering the addressee, the persuasion target.

Another slogan that does so is Burger King's "Have it your way." This is a slogan that bows to you, that says "You win." It also promises the whole world—unlimited wish fulfillment—by not promising anything specified and explicit. Recall the above discussion of "it" and "It is what it is." The implied meaning, of course, is that at Burger King you can have *your hamburger* whatever way you like. This is an important example of something we have not seen in the other ads, which is the main focus of the part of this book that deals with setting the agenda. Trying to take away market share from McDonald's, a thriving company that most customers were perfectly happy with, posed a daunting challenge to Burger King. How to do it? The answer was by taking what had been a neutral fact about McDonald's—its efficient, set menu and mechanized preparation process—and making it a liability; McDonald's cooks all its burgers *its* way, but at Burger King we welcome special instructions and variations; we want to do it *your* way. In practice, of course, there was very little difference between the two hamburger chains in terms of their flexibility and capability of responding to customer requests within the parameters of their range of ingredients and their cooking processes. In the realm of language and imagination, though, Burger King had

struck a resounding blow, by appealing to people's desires for freedom and for personal attention and special treatment.

Another agenda-setting slogan was M&M's "Melts in your
mouth, not in your hands"; in simply describing a feature of
this candy, where the chocolate is contained in a shell, the slogan simultaneously makes you conscious of something possibly
disagreeable about other chocolate candies, which is that if you
hold them without their paper wrapper, your hands will get gooey.
Since chocolate is something prized by almost everyone, making
it seem to be something disagreeable was a pretty good trick, but it
worked incredibly well.

Apart from the realm of advertising, we might consider some
more personal examples of breakthrough communication in politics and society.

Ronald Reagan, as a candidate for president, famously got a
great deal of mileage out of one moment in a primary debate in
1980. "I'm paying for this microphone," he said firmly, when the
debate moderator tried to cut him off; beyond the immediate context of the debate, the line got attention and resonated with the
idea that, like American taxpayers, he was not getting his money's
worth from the government represented by President Carter. The
moment crystallized very succinctly the mood of irritation with
taxes and government that Reagan had been working to place on
the national political agenda.

Barack Obama had a good moment in a debate during the
Democratic primaries of 2008. Congressman Dennis Kucinich
was on the same debate stage and was asked to comment on a past
incident where he had told friends that he had seen a UFO; this
story made Kucinich seem marginal, strange, and out of touch,
and his response of saying, in effect, "I saw what I saw" didn't help.
When the moderator turned the question to then-senator Obama,
"Do *you* believe in life on other planets?" Obama gave what some
later remarked was a perfectly pitched answer, which was to the

effect of "You know, I don't know. But I do believe in life on *this* planet. There are people on this planet who don't have jobs, who don't have health care . . . and those are the people we need to worry about first." His answer was, in a basic sense, respectful of the questioner but turned the question around in a way that exposed its triviality and allowed him to appear simultaneously grounded in real-life issues and able to think quickly on his feet. This debate performance may not have changed history, but it certainly did not hurt him in his ultimately successful campaign for the presidency.

Apple Founder and CEO Steve Jobs famously persuaded Pepsi executive John Sculley to come work for him by looking him in the eye and saying, "Do you want to sell sugar water for the rest of your life, or do you want to come with me and change the world?" Jobs's language was effective and succinct. His sentence structure ("Do you want to . . . or do you want to . . .") framed Sculley's situation as a choice between exactly two alternatives: one bad and one good. The option of remaining a Pepsi executive—something that many people might ordinarily consider a very respectable status— was lowered to "selling sugar water," while the option of working for Apple was translated into "changing the world." Sculley went to work for Apple.

The Irish rock singer and social activist Bono got involved with the Jubilee 2000 campaign, which was based on the idea that Western countries should celebrate the turn of the millennium by canceling the debt owed to them by impoverished nations of the world and especially those in Africa. Like a lot of rock and rollers, Bono can be outspoken on politics, and his views are often on the more liberal side of things. But he is also a committed Christian, and he was drawn to Jubilee 2000 because of its use of the biblical concept of Jubilee, which in ancient times involved the forgiveness of debts. A lot of people were surprised when Bono started hobnobbing with conservative Republicans in the U.S. government, but he knew that in order to have a true breakthrough and achieve results, he would have to reach beyond the liberal social groups that are usually interested in international aid projects. Bono later described to the English newspaper the *Guardian* how he had successfully advanced his agenda and achieved a positive outcome by finding common ground with the very conservative U.S. senator Jesse Helms: "He's a religious man so I told him that 2103 verses of scripture pertain to the poor and Jesus speaks of judgment only once—and it's not about being gay or sexual morality, but about poverty. I quoted that verse of Matthew chapter 25: 'I was naked and you clothed me.' He was really moved."

A somewhat similar story of successful outreach and persuasion in politics has been told by Harry Belafonte about his advocacy for the civil rights movement in the early 1960s. In a way that is similar to the case of Bono, Belafonte was already on the radar of the general public, including politicians, by virtue of his fame as a musical performer, and his intervening in politics was a matter of moving from one radar to another. The particular person whose radar he needed to get on at this point was the new U.S. attorney general Robert F. Kennedy, who had authority to enforce the law on a national level and was thus of great individual importance from the point of view of civil rights activists. The only problem was that Robert Kennedy at that time was better known for his participation in the House Un-American Activities Committee than for any known sympathy to the cause of civil rights. As Belafonte recalled in a radio interview, "When he became attorney general, with his record of anti-liberalism . . . it was a difficult moment for us. Dr. King, upon listening to all of us and how we criticized Bobby, said . . . 'Go out and find his moral center and will him to our cause.' And I think that that rather daunting suggestion challenged us, and we went out and did exactly that. We reached out to him and we brought him into our world, and we gave him the opportunity to look at what was happening" to the poor and to African Americans. The appeal that Dr. Martin Luther King Jr. made to Robert Kennedy, through the assistance of Harry Belafonte, is a textbook case of breakthrough communication, of finding common ground and bringing a person to share your agenda—and of having real results.

Another informative anecdote involved Robert Kennedy's brother, President John F. Kennedy. Around the beginning of the Cuban missile crisis, President Kennedy wanted to open a line of communication with the Soviet leader Nikita Khrushchev, and he did it in an unexpected way. Kennedy contacted his friend Robert Frost, the great American poet who had written a poem for his inauguration, and he asked Frost to go to Russia and meet with Khrushchev. It just so happened that the poet and the Russian leader both had a love for the greats of Russian literature— Tolstoy, Dostoevsky. Frost made the trip, even though he was 80 years old and sick. According to cabinet secretary Stewart Udall, who was there, Frost told Khrushchev that leaders had "a moral duty not only to steer clear of senseless wars but also to create a climate hospitable to wide-ranging contact and competition." Frost apparently made a strong impression on Khrushchev. No one can say for sure whether the visit contributed to the eventual resolution of the missile crisis, but again, some credit is probably due to President Kennedy for recognizing that a kind of common ground as seemingly obscure as an interest in Russian literature could become a focal point for connection with potential real-world consequences. Ironically, some of Frost's diplomatic work was undone when he got back to the United States and made a gaffe when speaking to the press at the airport; carelessly speculating that the Russians considered the United States "too liberal to fight," Frost gave the newspapers a controversial headline that embarrassed President Kennedy so much that it damaged their friendship. This too goes to show the importance of language and of never accidentally putting words in people's mouths, never losing sight of how other people (especially the media!) might frame what you say.

In the next chapter we'll look at how the concept of what I call "strategic" storytelling is transforming leadership and breakthrough communication in organizations around the world.

CHAPTER 10

Creating Meaning with Stories

One of my favorite assignments is the work we do with high-potential leaders from GE businesses around the globe. We conduct our workshops at GE's learning facility, called Crotonville, in Ossining, New York, just an hour outside Manhattan. Crotonville is the world's oldest corporate university—the first classes commenced in 1956. Nominated GE managers (you can't just sign up) attend various levels of executive leadership development and skill training programs and partake in the solving of real business challenges facing GE globally, hand-selected by the company's top leadership. Participants have to present their findings to other leaders at the end of such a program, with the potential that offered proposals can have wide-ranging impact on the business.

The Legends of Crotonville

The presentation part is where we come in. Toward the end of a particular program, my team of coaches and I arrive at Crotonville for three days to work with 56 leaders in smaller groups of 9 or 10, to prepare them for the presentation of their business challenge findings to visiting GE stakeholders.

One of the sessions we teach revolves around strategic storytelling and the leaders' ability to use narrative to connect their data to real-world consequences and, specifically, outcomes for people. Leaders learn how any number of objectives with an audience can be achieved by selecting just the appropriate story, based on proven story structures.

Like leaders in other industries and businesses, GE leaders need tools to overcome adversity, share knowledge so it sticks, engender trust, inspire collaboration, connect data to deeply held values, help others visualize a better future, and spark action for change. These are breakthrough communication goals that strategic and meaningful storytelling can help achieve.

One assignment we give GE leaders during our strategic storytelling sessions is to tell a story that has emotional resonance for them. We don't require that the story be a tragic, sad, or particularly happy one, but rather we ask that the story have deep meaning to the teller and have a clear point. As coaches, we look for authenticity in the way the leader tells the story, and we look for the structure that leads to a clear message.

One participant—we'll call him Mike—seemed uncomfortable when one by one his colleagues shared personally meaningful stories that occasionally brought tears either to themselves or to their peers, sitting in a circle around them.

When I asked Mike about my observation, he offered this: "I keep my personal life outside of work," and "I don't feel comfortable with going into personal stuff at work."

I told him it was okay if he wanted to sit this exercise out, and I asked if he saw value in the exercise for others, to which he responded, "Yes, sure, I can see how it connects people to one another," and "It definitely brings out empathy for others. I can also see how there are lessons that people have learned in these stories and how that can help others who face similar challenges."

When I asked Mike if he still wanted me to skip him, he said, "No, I'm good," and he got up to tell a powerful story of overcoming adversity.

There are a number of solid reasons for why narrative and story have such an impact and are the ultimate breakthrough communication tool. Human beings are conditioned from childhood to pay attention to and learn from stories. Stories help us get to know people on a deeper level through the shared human experience—what one person experiences, others can, on some level, empathically relate to. Stories, like those recounting the overcoming of challenges and adversity, give us hope and show us that no situation is hopeless. Stories can make sense of complex models and abstract concepts so everybody understands. Stories reflect life and tap into the experiences of others more easily in a way that raw data can't. Data and evidence may convince, but stories can weave them together to persuade. We also remember things better in the context of a story because our emotions are involved when we hear a compelling story. Particularly important for leaders, storytelling invites collaboration. The moment we hear a story, we can't help but visualize its message components in a way that's unique to us, becoming in a sense a cocreator of the story being told, rather than a detached observer.

Mike's story of overcoming adversity during our leadership communication workshop powerfully demonstrated the impact that sharing of specific experiences, and the choices we make in the face of adversity, can have on others.

"It was Christmas Eve," he starts out, "and like every 14-year-old kid in America, I loved Christmas . . . it was my favorite holiday. So I'm 14, it's Christmas Eve, and my Mom was murdered." He pauses for a moment before continuing, "Needless to say, such an event really changes you. But if someone asked me now, if you could go back, would you stop this event from occurring?

The answer I'd give is, of course, yes—and yet I profited greatly from it." Anticipating our reactions, Mike continues, "It sounds like a strange response. But the reason for that is . . . it shaped me for who I am today. And what it showed me is, that whatever adversity is put in front of you, you still have to figure out what your ultimate goal is and how to get to it. So, while I knew what my Mom wanted me to be as I progressed in life, it would have been easy for me to say, I'm going to give up. This tragic event has been put in front of me, and you know what, just throw in the towel. You have every reason to make an excuse and say here's why you can get off track . . . here's why you shouldn't be success-ful. But I used that as motivation. I knew my Mom wanted me to go to college. So you know what, I figured out how to pay for college. I put myself through four years of college, then went on to get a postgraduate degree. Why? It wasn't necessarily because I wanted to. It's because I knew my Mom wanted me to. And, realistically, I figured, hey, if I can do that . . . if I can go through something like that as a 14-year-old kid, there's nothing I can't face in corporate America. I've been through probably one of the worst events you can go through in your life . . . so everything else is easy. I wanted to share this story with the team, because, while this is adversity . . . I wouldn't change it, because it made me who I am."

The power of such an "overcoming-adversity" story is easy to grasp. We can empathize with loss. We feel inspired by the mental toughness and discipline it takes to get through such an event. We think about what we would do, and we see how one can indeed persevere during terribly difficult times. We see a role model, and at the same time we put our own challenges into perspective.

I'll point out here what should be obvious by now. The stories we tell in business and the professions should have a point, a mes-sage, a purpose. All too often, we hamper our own best efforts at reaching certain goals through storytelling—building rapport, among them—by doing it all wrong. We meander. We go verbose. We include unnecessary detail and go on tangents that bore people to death and build barriers rather than tearing them down.

For many of us who hold court at the water cooler, a letter of instruction written in the eighteenth century by the English nobleman Lord Chesterfield to his college-age son—a practice for which he became posthumously famous—can be enlightening:

> Do not tell stories in company; there is nothing more tedious and disagreeable; if by chance you know a very short story, and exceedingly applicable to the present subject of conversation, tell it in as few words as possible. . . . [N]ever think of entertaining people with your own personal concerns or private affairs; though they are interesting to you they are tedious and impertinent to everybody else. . . . Here people very commonly err; and fond of something that has entertained them in one company, and in certain circumstances, repeat it with emphasis in another, where it is either insipid, or, it may be, offensive, by being ill-timed or misplaced. Nay, they often do it with this silly preamble; "I will tell you an excellent thing"; or, "the best thing in the world." This raises expectations, which, when absolutely disappointed, make the relater of this excellent thing look, very deservedly, like a fool.

Motivating Others to Act

Aside from the inspirational overcoming-adversity story as illustrated by our friend Mike, there are other story structures that can help us create meaning in the minds of our listeners. Say, for instance, you want to motivate people to take certain action—the raison d'être of this book you're holding. This can't typically be accomplished with densely detailed stories that include the various twists and turns by colorful and varied characters we know from the movies and the literature of fiction. *War and Peace*, in all its storied glory, would be the wrong piece to motivate a crowd, even if every single detail and character in it is bursting with fascinating relevance to all kinds of things. As the storytelling expert and author of *The Springboard: How Storytelling Ignites Action in Knowledge-Era Organizations*, Stephen Denning, writes in *Harvard Business Review*, "I knew that in the modern workplace, people had neither the time nor the patience—remember executives' general skepticism about storytelling in the first place—to absorb a richly detailed narrative." Denning's research into the power of narrative for business purposes reminds us that, in order to be motivated, listeners have to be thinking about their *own* situation, their own life, their own needs, and they can't get too involved in the details of someone else's situation and problems. The best motivational stories are relatively brief ("Brevity is the soul of wit," says no less of an authority than William Shakespeare); they're simple, straightforward, and void of distracting and irrelevant details.

Think of this book as a case in point. In Chapter 8, I presented a series of what were in effect short *stories* designed to inspire and motivate you, the reader, to recognize and begin to actualize the hidden power of spin and framing in breakthrough communication. I told you the story of how Margaret Thatcher got Britain back on its feet; the story of how Gayle Trotter made a "feminist" pro-gun argument; the story of how King Henry V successfully rallied his troops to an all-but-impossible victory against enormous odds; the story of how Mark Antony got the people of Rome to reject the revolutionaries who overthrew Julius Caesar. None of these stories were overly long or complex, and all made a clear and simple point: somebody made a difference by taking some facts and framing them in a way that was different from the way they had been presented before.

In Chapter 9, I told you some more stories that could have significant motivational impact if you take them to heart. I told you the stories of how candidates Reagan and Obama, in their respective elections, seized a moment to say something profound that helped put them on track to win the presidency of the United States; the story of how Steve Jobs persuaded John Sculley to leave Pepsi and come to Apple with one simple, hard-hitting, and perfectly well-crafted question; the story of how the rock singer Bono found the common ground of religious belief to persuade the very conservative senator Jesse Helms that the United States should do more to help the poor in Africa; the story of how Harry Belafonte leveraged his status as a show business celebrity in order to get Robert Kennedy to pay attention to the civil rights movement and to support the activism of Dr. Martin Luther King Jr.; the story of how President John F. Kennedy leveraged the literary knowledge and wise reputation of the poet Robert Frost in order to communicate on a more human level with Khrushchev at a perilous moment in modern world history.

Did you see a pattern in the stories I told you in both of the chapters? If you did, it was likely the fact that these stories were, each in its different way, *success* stories, including a protagonist you could root for and identify with. According to Denning, these types of stories (he refers to them as "Sparking Action" stories) signal that a successful change took place—or not, in which case the negative consequences make the point of the story. These stories can work hard in sparking some kind of positive action from you, the listener; they are meant to inspire, to seek real-world accomplishments through the example of others who've come before and who've persevered in similarly challenging circumstances that favored the status quo. When you apply the principles of breakthrough communication and inject meaning into a story, you inspire others to help you achieve goals that are important to you and your organization. And the fact that the stories you read in the earlier chapters were short and got the point across succinctly underscores their applicability to the complex challenges we face at work with people every day.

Let's have a look at some of the narrative patterns Denning has identified as being useful for communicating for distinct outcomes. While Denning's story structures tend to overlap with one another and may be difficult to keep distinct—Mike's story above would fit into several of Denning's story structures—I offer examples below that should give business professionals plenty of context to draw from for their own stories or to find the right stories around them for adaption.

Engendering Trust

When an organization's frontline employees trust their leaders, they'll use whatever autonomy they have to find and implement better and more efficient ways of working in their jobs, according to business professors Gopesh Anand and Dilip Chhajed at the University of Illinois.

But trust isn't gained easily, or quickly for that matter. Whether we strike out on our own as entrepreneurs and engage in the daily struggle to connect with potential customers for our wares, or we work for an organization where we must lead others to reach important goals, without trust, we have little chance at success.

Can trust be generated with storytelling? If it's the right stories we tell, the answer is resoundingly yes. Let's say you are a new manager being introduced to your staff for the very first time. First impressions being as powerful as they are, you have a narrow but definitive window to let them know who you are, to convey something about your character, your ideas, your values, and your goals, not to mention whatever you think is the most important nugget of wisdom they should keep in mind as long as they are going to be working for you. At this point, you are *on the radar*; you are center stage; it is your moment.

Here, Stephen Denning advises a kind of emotional nakedness. Let people see you via a strength or vulnerability from your past, and let them know what lessons you've learned from that experience. For people to trust us, they have to know us on a human level, not just by job description or mission statement alone. Mike's story of perseverance in the face of adversity at a young age fits that bill. But as we've learned, it's often difficult for businesspeople who value professionalism over authenticity—though rarely is the trade-off clear to them—to present a more vulnerable side of themselves. We see that side of our clients in our workshops, but the transition of such honesty to the organizational day-to-day is a frightening mental leap for many.

Our political leaders, on the other hand, caught on long ago. They understand that for voters of all backgrounds to trust them, "the man and women on the street" must get to know the person behind the campaign posters on a personal level. Like candidate Bill Clinton, who told voters, as he ran for president, a story about how he finally stood up and defended his mother from an abusive second husband. Or like candidate George W. Bush, whose story to engender trust told of a religious awakening that, as an adult, gave him the strength to quit drinking at the time he came to the realization that he had a problem. Or like the story then-senator Joe Biden often recounted, about how his father always told him that the measure of a man is not how often he is knocked down but how quickly he is able to get back up. Let others peer into your life experiences and share the lessons learned, and trust by way of empathy may be a bit less hard fought.

Communicating Values

Values—it's a word we hear whenever a corporation strives to communicate what it stands for; it's a concept invoked whenever a political candidate or party hopes to appeal to voters, having done the polling and research necessary to identify shared values in its target audience. And for good reason—values and beliefs are pretty much what guide every decision we make. That's why, whenever we try to get a meaningful message across to our fellow man and woman, their value system will promptly spring into action to filter the incoming data, match the data against their own values, and then make a decision that either "feels right"—deciding in your favor or not—or "feels wrong"—causing a certain degree of cognitive dissonance. The latter happens when you make a decision that conflicts with your values, but you decide—for any number of reasons, e.g., to gain an advantage, to manage a relationship, to protect someone's feelings, to keep your job—to go against what deep down inside you hold as most important to you to guide you through life. Say you witness a colleague commit an immoral act at work, something that goes against everything you stand for, like honesty, integrity, fairness, ethical conduct, conscientiousness, and yet because you don't want to get your colleague into trouble or don't want to be seen as a snitch (also a value, though one you want to avoid), you keep quiet. This will cause you to feel disharmonious, thus producing cognitive dissonance. Conflicting priorities can be at fault here.

Another example is a doctor—a family man perhaps—who may feel cognitive dissonance as he works to save the life of a mass murderer who's committed heinous crimes against children. But by tapping into his deep professional values, among them *primum non nocere*, or "first, do no harm," he will have no second thoughts in saving the life of even the worst of human beings. So powerful are values in guiding our decisions, that ignoring them as we try to break through to others is tantamount to driving blindfolded on a busy highway—aimless and headed for a collision.

That we should learn about others' values before we can hope to resonate goes without saying. But a well-crafted story can provide a shortcut that shows others not just what's important to us deep down, but what we feel could be shared values that are fundamentally essential to all of us as human beings. This is particularly important if, as leaders, we want to reinforce or make known the guiding values of our organization that determine the cultural environment for a diverse group of people.

One story that conveys value and that has been told over many generations is the parable of the Good Samaritan. (Stephen Denning notes, in his *HBR* essay "Telling Tales," that value narratives are often in the form of a parable.) In fact, the phrase *Good Samaritan* alone carries the meaning of "somebody who does a good deed." What we may tend to forget is the original context of the story: the ancient Hebrews and Samaritans were enemies, so the idea that it was a Samaritan who came to the aid of the traveler would have been quite striking to the original readers of the Hebrew Bible. The story conveys the value of not being prejudiced, illustrating that we shouldn't necessarily buy into the idea that people will act a certain way simply because of the community from which they come. The power of these types of value-transmitting story is not simply in the core message they convey. It's that they also work in leaving some flexibility in the listener's mind to arrive at more personal meaning; some mental effort or "filling in the blanks" is helpful in making a story take root in the imagination of the listener. As Heather Forest has written, "It is empowering for a listener to make a creative leap and connect the metaphor of a story to the story of his or her own life. Recognizing and creatively processing an analogy is a way of personally embodying information as experience."

Generations of children around the world have been raised on the classic 1930 illustrated children's story *The Little Engine That Could*. In this story a large group of toys and dolls are stranded because their train broke down trying to carry them over a mountain. They wait patiently until a Shiny New Engine comes along. They ask for help, but the Shiny New Engine thinks it is too good for the job because it is a luxury passenger train, and so it won't help them. It goes on by, and then another train comes along, a Big Strong Freight Engine. Unfortunately, this Big Strong Freight Engine also thinks that it is too important for the lowly job of pulling a bunch of toys, because it is too busy with its important industrial work of hauling heavy equipment for the grown-up world. It too goes by, and eventually a dingy Rusty Old Engine pulls up. The stranded toys ask for help once again, but the Rusty Old Engine tells them that it is tired and needs a rest. "I can not. I can not. I can not," it says.

Then, finally, along comes a little blue engine chugging along cheerfully on the railroad track. The toys and dolls call out to it for help. At first the engine is unsure of its own ability to help them, since it is only used to help switch trains in the train yard and has never been over the mountain before at all, let alone haul any cargo. But the toys and dolls tell it, with tears in their eyes, that they need to get over the mountain before the little children on the other side of the mountain wake up and find that they don't have any toys to play with. So then the Little Engine gives the request a little thought and says, hmm, well . . . "I think I can. I think I can. I think I can." (Incidentally, what a lot of people may not remember, even if they've heard the story before, is that the Little Engine is referred to as "she.") So, *she* hitches herself to the broken train on which the toys and dolls are riding, and slowly she starts to pull forward, repeating, "I think I can. I think I can. I think I can" . . . until finally the Little Engine makes it over the crest of the mountain and brings the toys down safely to the children in the valley on the other side. They all cheer and thank her, and as she pulls away, they think they can hear the Little Engine saying "I thought I could. I thought I could. I thought I could. I thought I could."

As for the values that are baked into this time-tested children's book, they are obvious: chiefly among them, be willing to help, like the Little Engine did, and be willing to go beyond your comfort zone; give "it" your best shot, even if initially you are uncertain that you would be able to succeed. Perhaps, we could derive from the story the lesson that it pays to *tell* yourself over and over again that you think you can do something. In other words, it expresses the value of positive thinking and the importance of self-motivation in actualizing your potential by having a creed or an idea that you come back to and remind yourself of in times of uncertainty. We might also derive meaning from the idea that the Little Engine is a "she," and so we may conclude that it takes a girl or a woman to get the job done where others have failed to step up. You can see the meaning and values that kids can take away in such structured prose. For managers, business executives, MBA students, and others who are looking for stories to learn, present, or ingrain certain values, there are the case studies and the never-ending stream of news stories where people's decisions and actions point to their values, either honored or violated—think of NewsCorp's phone-hacking scandal—with corresponding consequences for all, played out in public. Whichever values you want to convey to others, make sure those values are clearly discernible from the structure and salient points of the story and are relevant enough to the particular situations of your audiences.

Getting People to Collaborate

The recently promoted executive managing director of a global data management company had a problem. With the transition into his new leadership role came a new team of direct reports who now worked alongside the team that had been with our executive for quite some time. It didn't take long for perceptions of favoritism and lack of access, by members of his new team, to take a toll on overall group morale, collaboration, and productivity.

That success in just about any venture depends on the collaborative efforts of many people and minds is hardly a secret. A secret weapon, however, may be what strategic storytelling can do to get people to work together and bond as a team with a common objective.

In the case of our data management executive, we recommended he get members of both the veteran team and the new team together in a meeting of the minds—with a very specific purpose—to tell stories. And not just any stories, but stories that centered on the common operational and managerial concerns they shared. With our executive moderating, the first member of the group started sharing some of the difficulties she and her team members were encountering, or had overcome, in the course of their work. The spark jumped over to the others, who were inspired to join in and share their own perspectives, difficulties, and challenges. Before long, aside from an important sense of shared purpose, camaraderie, and a general feeling of "we're all in this together," real solutions started crystallizing, with members of both "camps" vowing to support one another with resources and advice on the issues discussed. What individual conversations and halfhearted interventions behind closed doors couldn't accomplish before—the kvetching, gossiping, and finger-pointing only served to create more group divisions—the telling of meaningful stories could. The stories made progress possible; participants shared a sense of purpose and targeted the real issues they were facing. To be sure, our leader, who was at the center of the controversy, had to change his own behavior and work diligently to become more inclusive to avoid perceptions of special treatment and favoritism. But the strategic story sessions helped focus everyone's attention on critical objectives while creating awareness around the idea that a true team effort is needed with all hands on deck in order to succeed in the long term and to everyone's benefit.

Denning's research supports all this. He recommends that the stories shared—particularly the first one told in a session—"must be emotionally moving enough to unleash the narrative impulse in others and to create a readiness to hear more stories." To make efficient use of the energy and experience created by this type of storytelling, Denning supports creating an action plan immediately after to take advantage of the take-aways generated.

Managing the Rumor Mill

It's a typical scene around the proverbial water cooler or coffee-pot in any office: People casually gather in small groups and share the news and stories of the day. In more hushed tones, rumors are passed along; stories are created from fragments of information, and conjecture quickly becomes "fact." This type of social interaction has likely been going on since humans first gathered in caves, huddled around a warm fire. Add to this our relatively recent technological advancements and ubiquitous use of social media, and you've got millions of water-cooler conversations where information buzzes back and forth, from factual to completely fabricated. It's one thing to carefully craft and deliver the messages we need to get across as business leaders. It's quite another to anticipate and manage the informal chatter generated from even the most mundane organizational happenings. As Denning says, "The trick is to work with, not against, the flow of the vast river of informal communication that exists in every organization."

Particularly those rumors that have employees worried about their jobs, threaten the reputations of organizational leaders, or pit people and groups against one another can have troubling consequences. For leaders at any level, this means paying attention to the grapevine and being ready with counterstories to manage or swat down those rumors most potentially harmful to the organization. For an apt analogy we can revisit the topic of rhetorical spin and counterspin we discussed in Chapter 8.

If you remember from Chapter 8, Mark Antony created a counterstory to combat the story that Brutus and his friends had been putting out. Brutus and his coconspirators were essentially spreading the rumor that Julius Caesar was a tyrant who planned to make slaves out of the Romans, who had thus far been proud and free citizens; the conspirators' whisper campaign centered on the idea that Caesar was ruthlessly ambitious, which was why—for the greater good of Roman society—it had been necessary to kill him. This agenda might have taken hold in the public's mind—certainly Brutus and his friends were doing everything they could to infuse meaning into their narrative—except that Mark Antony was able to successfully pitch a compelling counternarrative. He resonated with the audience, making generally accepted facts about Caesar salient—that he was a great warrior, a generous man, and a good friend to the people of Rome—bolstered by authentic emotion and just the right amount of sarcasm.

It would be neither practical nor feasible for modern business leaders to respond to every single rumor that's circulating in an organization. It is imperative, however, to be aware of the narratives floating out there and to hone the proper instincts to know which ones to tackle. As a rule of thumb, if there's substance to a rumor, confirm what's true and add the necessary context to end counterproductive speculation. If a rumor is based on miscommunication or false information, make light of it, Denning advises—mocking either the rumor itself, the source of the rumor, or oneself to undermine the narrative's power.

Sharing Knowledge

At some point in our lives—whether we're business leaders or parents or teachers or mentors—we have a stake in sharing knowledge that needs to be retained, recalled, and potentially acted upon. To understand what narrative structures best facilitate the sharing of knowledge, we have to reflect on our own evolution. Think back to the teachers you've had over your lifetime—the good and the bad. Which stories made the material you needed to absorb come to life? When we remember individual snippets from the 24-hour news cycle, what was it that made the info stick to our intellectual walls? When a friend or colleague shares certain details with us, what do we remember weeks and months later? And why?

There is one fundamental characteristic that can make the sharing of knowledge via storytelling a successful endeavor, one that likely plays a role in the answers to the questions above. That characteristic is *emotional resonance*. Data, statistics, figures, and other factual information are more easily understood and recalled when we have an emotional response to the information. That's why people can often easily remember even the most mundane details surrounding an emotionally charged event, such as the attacks on 9/11, the night of the election of the first black U.S. president, or a natural disaster like Hurricane Sandy or Oklahoma's devastating tornados of May 2013.

In my workshops I often ask participants to share a personal story that is emotionally meaningful to them. Since these stories are always within the context of the material I am sharing, it is the participant's own story that anchors the new information for recall. Similarly, I make certain the anecdotes and stories I use tap into my audiences' personal experience and thus touch off an emotion that makes the information that's shared relevant, not just on a cognitive level but also on a visceral one.

To make this an intuitive practice, you may offer the following clarification and "heads-up" to those to whom you present: *"Here's what this means to you."* This simple sentence takes abstract concepts, say, self-control, weight loss, and exercise, and makes them meaningful by painting a concrete picture that evokes a certain emotion.

Case in point: A recent study from Texas Christian University had three groups of diners order from menus that listed either (1) the calorie count plus the amount of moderate exercise—say, 30 minutes of brisk walking—needed to work off the consumed calories, (2) just the calories for each food item, or (3) no health-related data at all. The study showed that people who had the concrete information about the specific exercise needed to work off the calories overate less than those who had either just the calorie counts or no health info at all. Visualizing ourselves sweating for half an hour to pay for an oversized bowl of pasta apparently hits us just where it counts, in the gut. The bottom line is, when we need to share information that matters, we need to tell the stories that have meaning to move people emotionally.

Leading People into the Future

Whether you have to persuade a teenager to go to college, a group of salespeople to hit a set goal, or a group of managers to adopt a new process, you have a particular future in mind, for yourself— if you have a stake in it—and for those to whom you speak. And it's that particular future state that requires the kind of story that sketches out a vision of the particular future that you desire to see, and more important, that you desire your audience—your employees or coworkers, for example—to see and work toward.

I'm reminded of a little story in which a pedestrian comes upon a man who is laying bricks. "What are you doing?" asks the passerby? "What's it look like?" comes the response from the bricklayer, "I'm laying bricks." As the pedestrian continues, he comes upon a second man doing the same work, and he asks him the same question. This time the answer is a little less hostile; "I'm building a wall," says the bricklayer. Finally the pedestrian happens upon a third man doing identical work to that of the other two bricklayers. When the pedestrian asks his question, "What are you doing?" the bricklayer beams, "I'm building a cathedral."

We can assume that the third bricklayer saw the future, the purpose for his hard work. Someone—his supervisor maybe or perhaps the commissioner for the cathedral—painted a picture of the future that gave the bricklayer a stake in it, i.e., personal pride in making this cathedral possible. A desired future state may not always be as clear-cut as a brick-and-stone cathedral, however. And the rewards may not be as tangible as that either. Which is why, Denning advises, we not be overly specific or predictive when we paint that image of the future, lest it turn out differently and end up disappointing and negatively affecting source credibility. Those of us in more senior leadership positions—including presidents and CEOs—are chiefly in the business of *inspiring*, creating pictures of the future that can endure.

And rarely was anyone more seriously in the business of leading people into the future and of crafting a vision for it than Abraham Lincoln. The famous words of his second inaugural address do just that—lay out a vision for how the United States is going to pull itself together after the Civil War finally comes to an end:

> With malice toward none, with charity for all, with firmness in the right as God gives us to see the right, let us strive on to finish the work we are in, to bind up the nation's wounds, to care for him who shall have borne the battle, and for his widow and his orphan, to do all which may achieve and cherish a just and a lasting peace among ourselves and with all nations.

Rarely was anyone ever more fond of telling a story, either, than Abraham Lincoln was, and there are countless examples of his storytelling with a practical purpose that would make for very useful study for any leader. But in the case of his inaugural address, notice that even though his vision is noble and majestic, it is also strategically vague: he says let us "do all which may achieve" peace with justice, but he doesn't give any specific policy proposals about that, partly because the situation is so vastly complicated and so fluid (remember the war is still going on at this point) that there is no way to sort out in advance what the best policy specifics are going to be. Abolitionists were furious with him for not saying whether the freed slaves would immediately be given full citizenship and voting rights; southerners were furious and fearful that he wasn't saying very much about *their* rights. But Lincoln was a pragmatist—he knew it would all have to be worked out later.

Unfortunately though, as we know, Lincoln didn't live to see it or to see it through. In Steven Spielberg's recent movie of Lincoln—where the dialogue is made up largely of Lincoln's actual words—there is a moment where Lincoln's son, who wants to enlist in the army despite his father's objections, says to him, "The war will be over in a month and *you know it will!*" Lincoln responds, "I've found that *prophesying* is one of life's less profitable occupations." Part of Lincoln's greatness as a leader and a motivator, as this movie truly captures, is that he didn't confuse offering a vision with making specific predictions, promises, or assurances when he knew that he couldn't know for sure what was going to happen. Whether you are telling a story that paints the future destiny of a whole nation or you are just telling a story to spark some smaller action, or communicate who you are, or transmit values, or foster collaboration, or tame the grapevine, or share knowledge, it is important, always, to respect the values and imagination of your listener. It is also critical to leave room and open possibilities in the story you are telling. Make it a story that can come to life, that can come true in the listener's mind, no matter what challenges and setbacks the uncertain future is going to bring. When people fill in the blanks and see themselves clearly in your story, they will muster the resources necessary on the way to that vision of success.

In the next chapter we'll look at what it takes to create that all-important spark and remain active when someone else finally agrees with you but hasn't acted in your favor yet.

Step Four

CHAPTER 11

Spark the Action
You Want to See

Now that presumably the first three steps have been taken effectively, it is time to consider the change in action, attitude, or behavior that you wish to see. There are barriers, and overcoming them is no small feat; it usually requires some spark, or active effort, on your part. In this chapter we'll focus on some of the more pesky barriers to change, and we'll offer some strategies for sparking action.

We may be convinced that smoking is bad for us—the countless studies and statistics are overwhelmingly clear, the mortality rates tell a sobering story, and the perceived social stigma of lighting up in public is just slightly less bothersome than being considered a drunk. And yet people continue to smoke.

In a similar vein, vast numbers of people continue to overeat despite irrefutable evidence and ubiquitous warnings about the dangers of obesity, not to mention the social and economic backlash against fat people. Southwest Airlines requires passengers who do not fit between a seat's two armrests to purchase an extra seat. Samoa Air—admittedly a small operation—puts individual passengers on a scale and charges them by weight. Public humiliation and major health risks notwithstanding, recent reports show that obesity continues to be on the rise in the United States, Canada, and Ireland, as well as other developed and emerging economies.

Heavy smokers and the obese know the stats, and though they are convinced by healthcare professionals, friends, and various media that they're on the potential fast track to a mortuary, they nevertheless fail to act on their own or even on their family's behalf. Convinced, we could say, but not persuaded.

Getting people to take action so that critical objectives—common or otherwise—can be met is the proverbial work we all have cut out for us. After all, breakthrough communication is about overcoming resistance and making things happen—getting results—through other people. Therefore, knowing the difference between convincing and persuading will not only distinguish the engaged reader from those who use the terms interchangeably— erroneously so—but move him or her, enlightened, from convincing to the next step of persuading. I'll give some quick grounding in the matter first, however.

Convinced Doesn't Mean Persuaded

Generally speaking, the important difference to keep in mind between *convince* and *persuade* is that *convincing* is rational and abstract, while *persuading* is emotional and practical. You may *convince* people of a proof in geometry or of the truth of some fact or theory, but you *persuade* people to *do something*, and you often accomplish this by appealing to their whole emotional being and world view, not just their rational bent. The word *convince* comes from the Latin *con* ("altogether") + *vincere* ("conquer or overcome," as in *invincible*). The word *persuade*, on the other hand, comes in similar fashion from the Latin *per* ("thoroughly") + *suadere* ("advise, recommend, urge as desirable"). Notice that this original word *suadere* is related to both *suave* and *sweet*; from this we can take the idea that you make something become *appealing* to someone. If "convincing" people means that you're "conquering" them, then you are not leaving any room for them as active, purposeful choosers or agents—they are just conquered or *defeated*.

There are some who'll undoubtedly feel a forceful argument should result primarily in a one-sided win. That's shortsighted, of course, as we don't want our customers, peers, employees, or bosses to feel *defeated* by our argument. Enlightened communicators strive for the opposite, namely to leave people empowered, uplifted, inspired, bought-in. This makes *persuasion* the nobler goal, as it makes people *want* to do the things you want as part of the whole of your objective.

Looking at the example from *Julius Caesar* discussed in Chapter 8, you might say that Brutus tried and failed to *convince* the people at Julius Caesar's funeral that they should approve of Caesar's assassination and support the assassins (or liberators, depending on whom you ask). Brutus gave rational arguments for this position, but his arguments failed because even though the people in the crowd at first partly agreed with him, they *took no action* as a result of his speech. Mark Antony, on the other hand, successfully *persuaded* the same crowd to reject Brutus and his gang. Antony, using storytelling, appealed to emotion, and he motivated the crowd to take immediate action; the crowd sent Brutus and his friends running for their lives.

What Are the Barriers That Remain for You to Achieve Breakthrough?

Let's consider other cases where people seemed to be convinced that an issue was important, but then no action was taken by, e.g., customers, clients, end users, citizens, or any other targets for the persuasion attempts. Change did not occur (at least initially) despite best efforts by the advocates. The challenges of radar, agenda, and meaning were successfully met, but the spark didn't ignite a fire. What happened? What's in the way? The reasons for preventing the spark from igniting a fire can be many. They may include (1) the issue of being *pleasing* or likable—a matter of taste with consumer products and a matter of relatability with people; (2) the issue of *timing*—partly a matter of luck, perhaps, but largely a matter of practical judgment; (3) the issue of *deciding* on an audience; (4) the issue of *understanding* your audience; (5) the issue of making people not just an audience but responsible participants or *stakeholders*; (6) the issue of establishing *trust and credibility*; and (7) the issue of *miscommunicating* or ineffectively communicating with the audience.

Barrier: Not Being Relatable or Likable

In the United States, where national politics is an ongoing, never-ending process, the two-party system somewhat reliably predicts that the failure of one side tends to be in a practical sense the success of the other. And the rhythm of things tends to be that one party's ideas are dominant for a while, after which there is a shift to where people tend to adopt the other party's ideas, and so it can be hard to pick out clear-cut, permanent stories of failure or success.

From the Republican Party's point of view, recent history includes the election of 2012, which must be considered a failure: the GOP (Grand Old Party) candidate Mitt Romney failed to seal the deal with American voters in spite of several factors that initially seemed to present significant advantages for him, including the sitting president's relatively low approval rating during the election (below 50 percent) and the relatively bad overall state of the economy, specifically including high unemployment. With Mitt Romney's personal background as an extremely successful businessperson, you might think he would have been able to parlay this American success story into a greater voter confidence on economic issues. But it did not prove to be so. Mitt Romney was definitely on the public *radar*, he had a very clearly articulated *agenda* in his party's platform, and he had some of the country's most skillful professionals helping him shape the struggle over *meaning* that involves framing issues one way rather than another way. But for all this, the spark was never lit (literally, as the media reported that Romney had purchased a $25,000 victory-fireworks display that had to go unused). It seems that Romney, for all his strengths, was never able to overcome the barrier of relatability—voters didn't have a problem with someone being as successful as Romney, but they were not finally persuaded that Romney could relate to anyone who wasn't as successful as himself.

This was a failure of Romney and his team to project the right personality, to have the right kind of credibility; and of course, the Democrats exploited this political weakness effectively. Too many voters just didn't "feel the spark" with Romney. What could he have done to change this? It's hard to say, since both personality and politics are complex concepts. But hypothetically if a campaign manager were to have focused on this issue with a more laserlike intensity, it might have made the difference. Certainly Romney's well-known dismissal of "47 percent" of the public as overly dependent on government seems to have had a dampening effect on popular enthusiasm for him, and it made it that much harder for any spark of support for him to catch fire and become change in his favor.

Apart from politics, we can look around us or look back through recent history and see other examples in the business world where the tipping point between failure and success was not successfully reached, where entrepreneurs did not achieve the breakthrough communication necessary to ensure the widespread embrace of their products by the public. If Mitt Romney was, in the end, simply not quite to the taste of most voters, he has this in common with many consumer products that have failed in the market because of a failure to come to terms with popular taste.

Coca-Cola Company had an embarrassing flop with its New Coke in 1985, and the company's great rival, Pepsi Co., had a similar failure with the introduction of Crystal Pepsi in 1993 and 1994. Jell-O Company, in the 1950s, discovered that there was very little public appetite for its experiment with a celery-flavored form of its product. In 1979, Clairol Hair Products introduced something called Touch of Yogurt Shampoo, hoping to capitalize on the general late-1970s popular interest in health foods; the product was a failure, though, because even though a lot of people liked yogurt and thought it was healthy, it just seemed a really bizarre idea to want to put yogurt in your hair. Specifically, the *barrier* here is one of resonance—the need to accommodate public taste.

Barrier: Having Poor Timing

New models of automobile, of course, can be hit and miss with the public. The most famous example of a miss is probably the 1959 Ford Edsel, which lost a few hundred million dollars for the Ford Motor Company—which was a significant amount of money in those days. One knock against it was that it was marketed as a flashy car, but it hit the market during a recession, when that was not what people felt they needed. The barrier was unfortunate timing.

Another area in which individuals with all the resources of radar, agenda, and meaning still frequently fail to motivate the action they want (i.e., sales) is in the communicative domain of filmmaking. A 1999 film called *The 13th Warrior* took on the interesting storytelling project of a kind of ancient multiculturalism, following the adventures of a man from medieval Baghdad as he travels north and encounters Vikings. This film failed to interest audiences at the time, and it ultimately lost $180 million; given that relations between the Middle East and the West were about to become of huge public concern with the September 11 terror attacks in 2001 and the Iraq War of 2003, it may just be the case

178

that this movie came out a few years too early. As with the Ford Edsel, the failure of this movie can be partly chalked up to timing. You might feel that timing is just a matter of luck, but I'd say that the less you believe in luck, the better. Timing is partly what you make of it. Ford would have been better off releasing the Edsel later when more people could have afforded it, or felt like they could. *The 13th Warrior* would undoubtedly have seen more interest if the film studio had released it a bit later.

Barrier: Failing to Determine the Audience

An additional problem with the Ford Edsel was that it was priced in a midrange; it was too expensive for most buyers, but it was not really a premium product either. Part of Ford's problem, then, seems to have been a basic indecision about whom it was trying to reach. The same might be true about another flick, the 2001 film *Final Fantasy: The Spirits Within*, which lost $164 million. It was technically innovative but was neither one thing nor the other; it was not realistic enough to please audiences interested in realism and not competitive as an animated film. The 2002 science fiction comedy *The Adventures of Pluto Nash* lost $124 million, basically because science fiction and comedy make somewhat conflicting claims on people's interest, and this film did not figure out how to blend them successfully. In all these cases, the barrier was the failure to *decide* upon or focus on the right audience.

Barrier: Failing to Understand the Audience

In 2001, similarly, the XFL (the name is analogous with NFL but with X for "extreme") was founded as a professional American football league by Vince McMahon, who is better known as the owner of World Wrestling Entertainment; the XFL was meant to be a hybrid that would appeal to fans of both NFL football and professional wrestling—a rougher, more show-biz and exaggerated form of professional football was the idea. The experiment never fully took off, though, partly because the things that people look for in the two sports are just basically different upon closer inspection. Marketing and framing bear some of the blame. XFL teams went for radical and extreme-sounding names to create a certain effect, but some of these backfired: the Birmingham Blast, for instance, was widely criticized for seeming to play on a 1963 church bombing in that city and/or a 1998 abortion clinic bombing there. The name of this team was changed, but the whole league failed to survive beyond its debut season. A 2009 animated film from Disney, *Mars Needs Moms*, lost $160 million—probably because Disney overestimated how much the moms in the audience were going to be interested in a film about Mars. The barrier that characterizes these examples seems not so much a failure to choose an audience as a failure to *understand* the audience that you have chosen.

Barrier: Failing to Engage the Audience

A memorable car-marketing failure besides the Edsel was that of the Yugo in the late 1980s, which was voted "Worst Car of the Millennium" by the popular radio program *Car Talk*, partly because of an easily overlooked maintenance requirement that would effectively kill the car after 40,000 miles if not carefully tended to. The barrier here is a failure to bring people on board, to give them ownership and a sense of responsibility. The Yugo was, after all, a good car for many purposes as long as it was properly serviced by an attentive and well-informed owner.

Poor engagement is also the culprit in the demise of lawn darts. In the 1980s, lawn darts were marketed as a popular outdoor recreational accessory; in the first eight years of that decade, though, over 6,000 people were treated in emergency rooms with lawn dart injuries. The product was eventually banned in the United States and Canada. Now, you might say that maybe this was just a case of an inherently bad product, but it's possible that the real problem was in the area of communication. Just as with the Yugo, the collapse of the lawn dart market might have been avoided and the darts might have remained a profitable product if the manufacturer had done a more careful job of creating an understanding of the ways in which the darts were and were not to be used. As well, the market for lawn darts might have been saved if the players had taken on a higher degree of responsibility for safety. Kitchen knives, after all, are much more objectively dangerous objects than lawn darts, but nobody has ever managed to ban or recall kitchen knives.

Barrier: Not Establishing Trust and Credibility

A major business debacle in this past decade was the decision by Bank of America in 2011 to charge a $5 monthly fee on debit card transactions. This was seen by many people as just too much, and Bank of America dropped the plan in short order. This is a case where a company misjudged a matter of pricing, but it is important to realize that there are also social, cognitive, and emotional factors in people's decision making and not just rationality or clear economic self-interest.

Another case of poor communication in business in 2011 was the decision by Netflix—as its business model was increasingly geared toward online content delivery—to redirect customers to a new website called Qwikster if they wanted to continue the established practice of ordering rental DVDs through the mail. This decision was reversed in less than a month after overwhelmingly negative public reaction. The initial decision, though clearly motivated by a wish by the company to enter a more profitable market sector, was unconvincingly marketed as something meant to make things more convenient for the customer—which, in fact, it did not do at all. Nobody was fooled, and many people were annoyed. Both Bank of America and Netflix stumbled over the same barrier: the issue of *trust and credibility*.

Barrier: Miscommunicating or Ineffectively Communicating with the Audience

In 1996 McDonald's brought out a hamburger called the Arch Deluxe, which was meant to appeal specifically to an adult market. The flavor of this sandwich was not hugely popular, and the price was generally considered to be too high—about twice the price of a Whopper at Burger King at the time. Another notable factor in the failure of this burger, particularly relevant to questions of communication, is that the $100 million advertising campaign that the company developed around its "adult" burger was misguidedly focused on emphasizing how unappealing the burger would be to children. This was a framing disaster that undercut the company's brand in two directions at once; it made it seem like the burger wasn't a pleasure to eat, and it also implied that the rest of the menu was food for kids rather than adults. Perhaps there is a cautionary lesson here about the effective use of *irony* in communication, which is surely part of what McDonald's was going for in order to seem "hip" or "savvy." The problem with irony is that it just says, "I don't really mean what I'm saying; I'm not serious about this," and it leaves the listener with no clear knowledge of what you *are*, in fact, saying and what (if anything!) you *are* serious about. As a result, it can backfire and harm one's credibility.

For another example of poor communication, let's go back to the realm of politics for a moment. A major attempt at gun control legislation—a major agenda item in U.S. politics—failed in the Congress in April 2013, despite strong presidential support and the apparent policy preferences of a majority of American citizens. Some will say that the failure of President Obama's gun control legislation was about money in politics—the National Rifle Association is so wealthy and influential a lobbying organization that no senators or members of Congress will dare to stand up to the organization. There is undoubtedly some truth to that, and it's a reminder that the most basic barriers to change are often simple economic realities—i.e., you just have less in the way of resources than your competitor or opponent. Nevertheless, it can't be denied that the NRA is not just a rich organization but a highly motivated one (and it is rich because its members are highly motivated contributors to it). The failure to effect change was therefore very much about ideas and communication and framing.

The fact is that gun rights advocates, as a politically active group, remain unpersuaded by whatever reasons have led most other Americans to support gun control. They are unpersuaded, even though they are quite aware of the gun-related tragic events that played out in the news, because they frame these situations quite differently. Instead of a fundamental abhorrence toward the idea of innocent people getting shot "all the time"—which is what likely motivates most gun control voters—gun rights advocates feel a fundamental abhorrence toward the idea of allowing the government to disarm them; they value freedom above all, and they believe that deadly force in the hands of each individual is the only way to preserve freedom. It is a major philosophical difference, and it is one not likely to disappear anytime soon. But for the sake of argument, if we put ourselves in the shoes of Obama and the Democrats, the barrier here is not just money but a particular mindset that would have to be changed, by effective communication, before political change could come about.

Obama obviously is on the country's *radar*, and the American people generally know (and in some cases mistrust) his *agenda* on this. The two hurdles that remain for him would seem to be *meaning* and *spark*, and these are, of course, interrelated, because in many cases what you need a *spark* for is precisely to make people see your side of things—your *meaning*—vividly enough to be persuaded to act in support of it. The journalist John Cassidy, in his interesting and provocative article "What If the Tsarnaevs Had Been the 'Boston Shooters'?," poses the question that if the Boston Marathon had been a *shooting* instead of a bombing, would that have provided the spark that was missing to pass Obama's gun control legislation? The event itself might have constituted the spark on one level, but the bill's supporters would have had to also work hard to make the connection meaningful enough in voters' minds.

We have seen a number of possible barriers to breakthrough communication. Sometimes people simply won't be persuaded because of any number of biases, preconceived notions, cultural differences, misunderstandings, competing or conflicting priorities, etc. And as we'll work out in the following chapter, the issue of managing fear is one of the truly most important aspects of outcome-oriented breakthrough communication.

But before that, I'd like to highlight several tools for sparking action and change, as advocated by one of the world's most respected scholars on the topic of mind change.

What Causes Change to Happen?

Harvard Professor Howard Gardner, in his book *Changing Minds*, lays out and argues for a multipronged approach to mind change with his seven "levers."

Reason

In some contexts, this is the principle that is going to carry the most weight—in an academic setting, for instance, and in many high-level policy discussions, reason is really given its due value as a means or mode of persuasion. Pure intellectual reason, as a tool of persuasion, might perhaps have been applied more effectively in several of the cases considered above: the Arch Deluxe sandwich, the Yugo, the lawn darts, and arguably also the gun control debate. In each of these cases, the persuasion target was the public, and some form of public well-being was at stake. To a certain extent, it simply stands to reason that one would want to eat healthily, service one's car effectively, use outdoor toys safely, and minimize the chance of being killed by a gun in the hands of a criminal or a mentally ill person. Reason means thinking things through logically and expressing them logically, and doing so in each of these cases is very much a matter of conceptual framing. "Frames," as it turns out, are how we *think*, not just how we persuade each other. Using frames well means both thinking well and persuading well.

Research

Research is, of course, closely connected with reason—the empirical or scientific connected to the rational—and both are used and appreciated in academic and policy contexts. An example of change coming about through research—and effective communication of that research—could be found in the fact that smoking has declined in the United States and many other countries in the last few decades, thanks in large part to rigorous scientific studies establishing the true health consequences associated with tobacco. A similar if only slightly less dramatic example could be found in the fact that when research showed there were harmful effects from using trans fats as a food additive, the FDA required that the effects be listed on food packaging, and many food-producing companies opted to remove the trans fats rather than create a negative impression on the customer. In this case, scientists like Dr. Walter Willett of the Harvard School of Public Health first used their clout to get trans fats on the *radar*, to further their *agenda* about them, and to establish their *meaning* (i.e., not that they were a tasty and effective preservative, which was what they meant to the food industry, but that they were a substance that built up in the body with damaging and often ultimately fatal effects). Their high-profile lobbying of the FDA to introduce warning labels provided the *spark* that produced voluntary change in the industry.

Representational Redescription

This is the term that Howard Gardner uses for the idea that changing people's minds can be a slow process, and that it is, in effect, a battle on many different fronts at once: spoken words, writing, images, modeling behavior, etc. One example that comes to mind here would be Barack Obama's successful first presidential campaign of 2008, which brought about change (and "Change" was, famously or notoriously, the campaign slogan) at least insofar as it put a Democrat rather than a Republican in the White House. This campaign was multimodal and operated on a variety of levels. There were slogans, speeches, photo ops, carefully planned graphic design artworks, and extensive use of digital media. There was an appeal to voters who were tired of the policies and style of President George W. Bush. There was an appeal to young people who could relate more easily to the youthful Obama than to his rather elderly Republican rival, Senator John McCain. There was an appeal to historical consciousness with the prospect of electing the first African American U.S. president, and there was a related invocation of civil rights iconography, from Obama's announcing his campaign in the same place that Abraham Lincoln did, to his frequent quoting of Dr. Martin Luther King Jr. In all, the campaign was probably successful in large part because of the way it mobilized many different media and messages toward a common purpose of persuasion. Obama, as a senator, was on the *radar* and had an *agenda*; he and his team went to work on many fronts at once, to establish the *meaning* they wanted in people's minds. The *spark* was lit not just one time but over and over again during the course of a long campaign—starting perhaps with the 2004 keynote speech at the Democratic National Convention that first brought him a national spotlight and continuing through all the significant communication turning points of his subsequent career.

Resources and Rewards

These are one way of affecting people's behavior without necessarily changing the way they think. It is a truism that "money talks"; yet there are some limits to the power that this "lever" can have: President Obama was reelected, after all, in spite of the unlimited money that the Supreme Court's 2010 *Citizens United* ruling allowed to be spent against him by large corporate donors who, by and large, lean Republican.

Real-World Events

A critical spark for mind change may come in the form of our response to events that are occurring in the world around us. The Sandy Hook school shooting of December 2012, for instance, caused many people to look with favor on proposed gun control measures they had previously opposed. The Boston Marathon bombing affected saliency in public debates about immigration, education, profiling, etc., and it remains to be seen (as of October 2013) whose agendas it will ultimately have furthered as a spark— depending upon which group proves most adept at framing its message. Events are "the hand you are dealt," and it is up to you to decide how to play it. They are what make the factor of *timing* (as with the Edsel and *The 13th Warrior*) either a barrier or an opportunity.

Resonance

This is when change comes about due to emotional factors more than strictly rational ones; we saw one good example of this in Chapter 8, where Mark Antony's emotional appeal to the people of Rome ended up carrying more weight with them than his rival Brutus's appeal to their rational thinking. A well-known key factor of successfully changing minds is to be perceived as trustworthy and likable. Mark Antony used those qualities more effectively than Brutus did in the year 44 BC, and arguably President Barack Obama used them more effectively than former Massachusetts governor Mitt Romney did in the U.S. presidential election of 2012. The film *The 13th Warrior*, I have suggested, might have resonated better with potential audiences if it had come out right after, rather than right before, the events of 2001–2003, during which Americans found themselves having to come to terms with Middle Eastern cultures in conflict situations.

Plenty of failures in the annals of business can be chalked up largely to problems with resonance. People didn't really dislike the taste of New Coke so much as they disliked the *idea* of a new Coke recipe—Coke was as traditional a piece of American identity as you could find anywhere; you might as well choose new colors for Old Glory. There's no obvious reason you couldn't enjoy celery-flavored Jell-O; after all, a lot of people buy celery, or it wouldn't be in the stores. And yet there was something about it that just didn't resonate; people want desserts that are desserts, and they want health foods that are health foods. They also don't especially care to put health foods in their hair, as Clairol found out with its Touch of Yogurt Shampoo. The XFL didn't resonate with the public very well because the vibe of professional wrestling is really pretty different from the vibe of professional football.

Resistances

People have a strong natural tendency to hold on tightly to theories and stories they have always accepted. *Recognizing and understanding* resistance is consequently a lever of the utmost importance for anyone who wants to bring about change. Often the best-qualified people to overcome resistance in skeptical audiences are those who are known to have experienced resistance themselves. This is what is meant by the statement "Only Nixon can go to China"; President Richard Nixon, as a Republican and longstanding Cold War critic of Communist China, had credibility as an American leader who could be trusted to uphold America's interests in its new dealings with China in the 1970s; his visit to China was a *spark* that enabled change. Resistance to change is a fact of life, and it is important for would-be communicators not to despair when such resistance is strong; instead it is essential to take a long-term view, chipping away at the resistance bit by bit. Much of this chapter has been devoted to considering different factors that can offer resistance to change, but a good grasp of Gardner's seven levers is an invaluable way to see to it that change, rather than resistance, has the last word.

In the next chapter we'll discuss the topic of managing fear. When change occurs, negative emotions are bound to accompany it, either in the target of your communication efforts or perhaps in those who work with (or surround and influence) the target. This is part of the breakthrough communication process.

We'll look at ways to manage fear within that process.

CHAPTER 12

Managing Fear

This four-letter word—*fear*—deserves its own chapter for its formidable role as gatekeeper to many of the things we want in life. Whether it's our own fear that, for myriad reasons, keeps us from speaking up for our ideas and beliefs, or the fears of others that keep them from acting on our best suggestions and proposals, breakthrough communication is hard to achieve when the emotion of fear isn't managed effectively.

What are *you* afraid of?

Chances are that when you reflect on this question, you come up with a few things that range from mild-anxiety inducing to sheer terror. The old chestnut of "public speaking being feared more than death itself" comes to mind. Phobias from fear of heights, to fear of spiders, to fear of flying are part of everyday conversation. And who doesn't know someone who's terrified of the dentist? There's probably a dentophobe within your own family.

While fear is a perfectly natural emotion that primarily serves as a self-preservation mechanism—it's what keeps most of us from strolling through dark alleys in rough neighborhoods—it can just as easily turn irrational and keep us from taking advantage of any number of career-boosting opportunities, such as presenting our best ideas to decision makers in our organization.

Questions torment us, like "What if I look foolish?" "What if they think it isn't my place to suggest this idea?" "What if they think it's a dumb idea?" "What if I'm misunderstood?" Then we start rationalizing: "This probably isn't a good time." "If I get shot down, I'll be humiliated." "Nobody else says anything; I won't stick my neck out." When fear controls people's actions, innovative ideas remain in the heads of their creators instead of being thrown into the mix for consideration and critical analysis.

Then there are the consequences that hit closer to home. Not simply a nuisance, but rather a real problem in pediatric dentistry, is the fear that is associated with the earlier alluded-to trip to the dentist. Imagine the frightened child who's loath to sit in that chair, a towering adult aiming a high-speed drill at his wide-open little mouth. The child doesn't know what's happening, so he looks to his parents for reassurance.

And that's where the fear takes root, because research shows that it may be you, the parent, who has saddled the little ones with fear and terror. As a *Science Daily* report notes, a recent study "confirmed that the higher the level of dentist fear or anxiety in one family member, the higher the level in the rest of the family." Such fear might lead to appointment cancellations, refusals to cooperate, and, of course, the decision to avoid the dentist altogether.

The good news, if you're that parent, is that you can help your kids with breakthrough communication in overcoming that fear of the dentist, the end result being regularly scheduled, fuss-free trips to the dentist, not to mention better dental and overall health.

You are in the perfect position to achieve this: you are clearly on the *radar* of your children, and you also have source credibility to set the *agenda* and determine what gets talked about. Your kids, incidentally, don't. While many parents may unconsciously use complaining language and speak in terms of their own fear of the dentist, you can influence how your kids think by speaking in more positive terms about a dental visit, thereby changing its meaning. Rather than talking about how much you hate the high-pitched noise of that drill when it grinds down on that molar, sending mist and enamel shrapnel flying through your mouth and the air in front of it, all while feeling the drill's tip coming closer and closer to the nerve, you could be creating an altogether different kind of expectation. You might comment on the friendly hygienists who hand out brand-new personal toothbrushes and give you headphones so you can listen to music or watch a DVD, as well as the fresh and clean feeling you take away from the checkup and the joy and confidence you get from a healthy smile. By making positive aspects of the visit salient, you can change the perceptions the kids have, simply based on how you talk about the experience.

It's not just about the words you use, however. Your nonverbal language is on full display and may betray an insincere attempt. Children can pick up when their parents are obviously faking it: a tight smile or a quivering voice is often a dead giveaway that statements like "This will be fun!" or "There's nothing to worry about" mean the opposite. Thus, enhance your reassuring words with a calm approach. "With regard to assistance in the dental clinic, the work with parents is key. They should appear relaxed as a way of directly ensuring that the child is relaxed too," study author América Lara Sacido states. "Through the positive emotional contagion route in the family, the right attitude can be achieved in the child so that attending the dentist is not a problem."

You've now changed the meaning of a dental visit by focusing on comfort and reward versus pain and inconvenience. By maintaining a consistent *salience* and *meaning* focus around the dental visit, you can break through the fear barrier via your communication and spark change, such as buying into future dental visits, keeping appointments, and following the dentist's routine instructions to "brush your teeth."

Getting a Grip on Fear

The dental visit study shows how our own fear, if not managed properly, can influence others to behave in undesirable ways, not only to their own detriment, but with far-reaching consequences for all involved. Think of a military leader in charge of leading troops during a dangerous mission. Were this leader to show fear in uncertain situations that call for clearheaded decision making and displays of courage, it could prove disastrous for the leader himself and those under his command. Think of a first-responder firefighter who instead of showing calm and confidence in an evacuation situation dissolves into an emotional breakdown while trying to guide frightened victims to safety. Such behavior would most certainly escalate the fears of those who are most vulnerable in situations of great peril.

The complex world of business itself has innumerable opportunities where displays of courage and confidence will win the day over fear and timidity every time. Just think of a manager who, giving a presentation to assembled executives, falls apart at the first signs of impatience by her bosses or, worse, an attack during a spirited question-and-answer session. Or picture the business leader who breaks out in a cold sweat during negotiations that make a deal seem less and less likely as the talks go on. The outcome will rarely be good.

No leader, no professional communicating for a breakthrough, can afford to let fear take the upper hand when clearheadedness, compelling arguments, and confident delivery are what others expect and need.

So how do you calm yourself when you feel fear creep in, so that others maintain their confidence in you?

Practice Self-Awareness

Many of us are more afraid of the emotions of fear than of the "thing" that triggers the fear itself.

Notice what is happening to you. Take note of the physical symptoms as if you were a detached observer. Check in with your body to see what it's doing. Are your knees feeling weak? Are your palms sweating? Do you feel perspiration on your forehead? Is your mouth getting dry and your breathing more shallow?

By quickly getting a picture of and focusing on the physiological response in your body, you are interrupting the thought process that sparked the biological response in the first place. An important next step is to tie these physiological manifestations of your emotion back to the thoughts that caused them. By understanding the connection, you have a clear picture of what causes the fear and can assign a more appropriate response to the cause, as opposed to leaning into the panic that normally befalls you.

You can try this right now. Think of an issue that is currently causing you distress and observe your emotional response. You might start feeling sad, angry, disgusted, or fearful. Now focus on the physiological response in this moment. You may notice a lump in your throat. You may feel your pulse racing. You may notice your facial expressions changing, like your eyes narrowing, your jaw clenching, or your lips pursing. Maybe there's a pain in the pit of your stomach. Whatever your response, your focus on the physiological manifestation of your emotions will temporarily suspend your thinking about the source of your emotions. That's because we simply cannot focus on two things at the same time. We can switch back and forth, but we can't focus on more than one thing at a time. Practicing being in the moment and having full awareness is your first step in the process of calming yourself. And as you'll notice, taking focus from the source of the emotion of fear weakens the fear. Your next step is to get some perspective on the sources of your fear response.

Gaining Perspective

Aside from focusing on and thereby interrupting the emotions of fear in the moments of fright, we need to put in perspective the issues that cause us to act out of fear.

For most of us, fear is a psychological phenomenon that springs from one or several narratives we tell ourselves about the future or the past. We might worry ourselves sick about an upcoming meeting with our boss. Or we might fret about a presentation we gave that didn't go as we'd hoped. We continually create negative stories in our minds that support our feelings of dread—always ending in the worst possible scenario.

Compare this with the fear we feel when we're in a car with someone who is driving fast and recklessly. Or the terror we'd undoubtedly feel if we were to face a big growling dog, off its leash, preparing to charge at us at any moment. The fear we feel in the latter scenarios is arguably useful, as we'd likely tell the reckless driver in no uncertain terms to slow it down, while making use of the fight-or-flight mode our body is in as we face the ferocious dog. In that case we either run and leap over the nearest fence or, possibly, determine that we can fight the dog off. In either situation, the fear is justified and helps us act decisively.

Not always is fear this useful, however.

The German-born spiritual teacher and author Eckhart Tolle teaches in his book *Practicing the Power of Now* that "the psychological condition of fear is divorced from any concrete and true immediate danger."

To differentiate between "psychological fear" and the fear that usefully alerts us to *real* danger, we have to gain perspective.

Say it's a meeting with the boss you're worried about; what can be done to manage or eliminate the fear that is unproductively occupying your mind and making you feel discomfort?

If you don't know what the agenda for the meeting is, you could ask. I'm often surprised at how many people simply choose to suffer in the anguish of negative anticipation rather than ask the simple question, "What is it that we'll be discussing at our meeting?" or something to that effect. If you get a straight answer like, "I'd like to talk about your handling of the Johnson account last week," you can now anticipate certain questions and prepare, if necessary, a case that supports your handling of that account. Or you might gather additional data that will prepare you for an intense Q&A session on the issue with your boss. Either way, you're changing the focus from fear of what the boss might want to talk about to a mindset of productive anticipation and preparation. If the answer to your question is less illuminating, focus on the present moment, which is the only time you can actually do your best work—you can't do your best work in the past or the future. This way you will also take the focus off the negative narratives you tell yourself about what might happen in the upcoming meeting.

Of course, it isn't just possible future events we worry about. Doubts and anxiety about the past can be just as disconcerting and cause fear to disrupt our best communication efforts.

If you are worried sick about the consequences of a presentation you just gave that didn't produce the results you hoped for or went off the rails somewhere along the way—that too is a psychological fear that can be managed so you can restore mental balance.

By conducting a postpresentation analysis, ideally right after your talk, you can quickly identify where you might have done better based on audience feedback (or lack thereof) and use that information to improve your next presentation. To do this in the most effective manner possible, check in with peers or audience members you trust to give you an honest assessment of where you provided value and where you failed to do so. Make certain you capture all relevant information to correct course for the next scheduled talk.

Confide in a Friend

Sounds simple enough, but if you've ever shared a personal fear with a friend, you know that the old saying "A problem shared is a problem halved" has merit. The German equivalent is "Geteiltes Leid ist halbes Leid," meaning shared suffering is half the suffering. Both point to a kind of relief from fears and concerns once they're shared with someone else. It isn't only the act of sharing alone that provides benefit, as another's perspective can put things in, well, proper perspective. Confiding in a friend can take the sting out of an issue we ourselves are perhaps too close to and may have blown out of proportion.

The effect of this can be multiplied by sharing with more than one trusted advisor or friend and getting the benefit of multiple viewpoints—and with that, possible solutions to what might be an easily solvable problem.

Focus on Your Strengths

Whether we are in the midst of a heated question-and-answer session in the corporate boardroom or are otherwise stumped or intimidated by others we deem much smarter than ourselves (it happens), we do have our strengths to fall back on. Imposter syndrome—the feeling that one is a fraud and does not deserve the position one is in or accolades one receives—is reportedly a common affliction even in top management circles; however, it pays to reflect on one's accomplishments. Humility is a wonderful trait and key to emotionally intelligent leadership, but an objective assessment of our worth and value to an organization, a cause, or a team is critical to chase away the fear of being inadequate. While we may not have all the answers in a given moment— do offer to provide them in due time—we should reflect on the reality that what we *do* know has gotten us to this point, and we deserve to be here.

Determine to Provide Value

My advice here is closely related to the speaking-in-front-of-groups fear, and that advice is *always provide value*. We often fear things when we feel we are inadequate or unprepared or ill equipped to meet certain challenges. By determining to provide others with real value and focusing hard on making that happen, it is hard to focus on any psychological fear of being irrelevant. Clearly defining to ourselves and to others what value we are providing and how it affects lives for the better, along with getting confirmation that this is indeed so, is one of the best antidotes to fear and is a boost to the confidence that makes others look up to us.

Helping Others Manage Their Fear for Breakthrough Results

Even as we manage our own fears in order to confidently and compellingly communicate important messages to others for any given objective, we will find that *their* fears are often in the way of making things happen.

When this is the case, when fears thwart the people who can help us, we need to use empathy, skill, and patience to help them overcome those fears.

We should ask ourselves whenever we are hoping to break through to people: "What are their fears with regard to what I am asking of them?" "What keeps them up late at night that stands in the way of their taking action?" "What are the risks from their perspective?" "What could they lose if my ideas are accepted and acted upon?"

An article by Chloé Morrison highlights a recent survey on workplace fears by Accountemps, a division of staffing giant Robert Half International. The study, according to Morrison, finds that the top fears in the workplace include the fear of "making a mistake," the fear of "difficult consumers or clients," and the fear of "conflicts with a manager," followed in rank order by the fear of speaking in front of groups and conflicts with coworkers.

Of course, anyone in business and the professions has likely encountered symptoms of other fears that stand in the way of breakthrough communication, such as the fear of change, the fear of being judged, the fear of making decisions, the fear of being left out, the fear of office politics, the fear of not being able to keep up, and the fear of losing control, among a long list.

Any one of these fears, not to mention a combination of them, can stop our best communication efforts in their tracks, unless we can help our targets for breakthrough communication overcome their fears. And while this is anything but easy, there are principles that can be applied to reduce the symptoms of their fears and give your proposals, suggestions, and messages a fair shot.

I'd like to give you at least one breakthrough idea for each of the above mentioned top fears. Add these fear-busting techniques to your communications arsenal so your messages can spark the desired actions, unencumbered by fear.

Making a Mistake

According to the Accountemps survey, this fear tops the list in the workplace at close to 30 percent. You, as either manager, peer, or even direct report to someone who has this fear, can have a positive impact on the afflicted.

When people are worried about making mistakes, they usually fear repercussions. As manager of a unit or leader of an organization, you can influence the overall culture by letting it be known that without experimentation, trying new ideas, and going out on limbs, innovation and progress will be hard to achieve. You can tell stories that include protagonists who, in pursuing a better way of doing things, discovered instead what doesn't work, with important lessons learned along the way. You can tell anecdotes of success where taking a risk resulted in making new discoveries and creating new opportunities. And if you're in charge, you must make it clear that not only are people encouraged to take risks, but they are rewarded for doing so, as opposed to being punished when the outcome is not what was hoped for. Actions speak louder than words, and as a leader of people, you have to demonstrate and practice what you preach. Be aware that what might be perceived as "punishment" for honest mistakes can undo your message and reinforce in others the fear of making mistakes.

So if your message is one of innovation and action and experimentation with new ideas, let people know—in word and deed and via multiple media and message channels—that it's okay to make mistakes for the sake of learning better ways in the process. Also point to examples and evidence that bolster your message. And if you aren't in charge, but rather are dealing with this fear in your bosses or peers, you can use similar stories and evidence that show how making mistakes is the only way to find better solutions, while reminding the brass that punishing those who explore different options that may or may not work out will only lead to stagnation and reinforce the status quo. Challenge those leaders to show you successes that came about without useful mistakes having been made along the way.

Remember, just as with establishing the agenda and regardless of your organizational status, you must have source credibility in order to successfully convey this message—meaning do your homework and learn about the lessons and mistakes made by the most admired business leaders, innovators, political leaders, and humanitarians that enter our conversations: Jobs, Branson, Welch, Clinton, Blair, Zuckerberg, Immelt, Greenspan. Look especially at the key figures in your field and pull the stories that make them human as opposed to godlike.

Difficult Consumers or Clients

If you're working with someone who's afraid of dealing with difficult people, you need to help that person put things in perspective and see issues from a customer's or client's point of view. All too often we take frustration or outbursts by a customer or client personally. Instead, help others learn to get an accurate understanding of their customers' needs and feelings. Encourage them to listen to and focus intently and without judgment on someone else's experience and concerns. People may find that the threat of difficult customers often disappears when they separate the signal from the noise, giving them the satisfaction of truly being able to help solve customer problems.

Conflict with a Manager

If you're the manager, you can contribute a great deal to eliminating this fear in your people. Get to the root of the conflict and hear people's concerns. Invite open and honest dialogue. Look for solutions that consider all sides of an issue and that respect others' concerns. The opportunity to remove the obstacle of fear when you're in a position of power is great.

In one of my executive coaching sessions with a senior leader at General Motors, the client confided in me that he was no longer enjoying his job and that in the 30 years he'd been there this was the worst he'd ever felt. The reason—conflict with his boss, whose office his was next to. Over the course of months, his boss routinely dressed him down in front of others in meetings and generally acted frustrated with my client, to the point where Jim (name changed for confidentiality) hated coming to work in the morning at the company he loved. I asked him the source of the conflict, and he didn't know. I wondered aloud if he had sought to speak with his boss about this climate of conflict, and he answered that he hadn't. It was as if fear and a feeling of defeat had robbed him of his spirit. Upon my suggestion, Jim approached his boss the next day and started a dialogue in which he stated how he was feeling about their relationship and what impact it had on his morale and those reporting to him. He asked for clarification and got it. In the process, important issues and emotions that had been left unspoken came to the surface and had the chance to get resolved. Jim's boss appreciated his reaching out and opening the dialogue. After a few days I received a brief e-mail from my client that read, "Harrison, our conversation the other day was life-changing. Will fill you in."

You don't have to be an assigned coach to help people overcome the fear of conflict with a manager. Just by suggesting they start communicating with their manager about how they feel with the intent of resolving any pending issues and by letting them know they have your support, you can help peers and others in your environment overcome their fear of conflict with a boss.

Speaking in Front of Groups

Together with my colleague Dr. Larina Kase, I have written an entire book on this topic, *The Confident Speaker.* My short but substantive recommendation for you to help others conquer this fear (other than giving them a copy of our book) is to remind them to (1) have a firm objective before getting in front of an audience; (2) know the listeners and their needs and concerns better than the listeners themselves could articulate them (this is done through research); (3) give tangible value to the audience, perhaps phrased and repeatedly offered as "Here's what's in it for you"; (4) maintain a consistent focus on providing tangible value throughout a talk, which will minimize self-consciousness, i.e., self-focus; and finally, (5) solidly prepare, keeping in mind one overriding goal: getting a clear and simple message across to people that compellingly illustrates how their lives will be impacted (it is hoped, in a positive way). By following these guidelines and keeping the focus on audience value during the talk, fear can be converted to the positive energy that fills us when we are truly invested in helping people.

Conflict with Coworkers

While it doesn't rank as high as the fear of conflict with a manager, fearing conflict with coworkers can close people to important insights from others, not to mention stifle collaboration and transparency in the workplace. An atmosphere of fear among coworkers may be one of the most destructive manifestations of fear there is and a real detriment to organizational climate, not to mention business success.

Similar to the situation of conflict with a manager that I described earlier, helping someone overcome the fear of conflict with coworkers requires the courage to take the first step and approach others with an open mind and willingness to truly listen to any issues at the root of the conflict. Any misunderstandings and prior miscommunication can then be brought to light and discussed. Depending on the root cause of the conflict, a mutual agreement by the parties involved, to put organizational values first and find common ground, can help put fears to rest and focus on what's truly important.

When another coaching client, an HR leader for Hewlett-Packard in the Asia-Pacific-Japan region of the organization, was promoted to lead a team of former peers, he was initially reluctant to address individual conflict situations that stemmed from his change in status and a different leadership style than the team was used to. He chalked the conflict up to jealousy and avoided confrontation for fear it could escalate. After some consideration, and some gentle prodding on my part, he resolved to approach the former peer whose behavior had changed markedly since my client's promotion, and he invited her for a chat over coffee. During their conversation he was able to appreciate his colleague's perceptions and concerns with several new policies he had set and to add clarity and context where previously speculation and conjecture led to barely concealed hostility. The end result was a fresh start for both parties and agreement on frequent feedback and open communication.

These are a few solid ideas you can use to help others overcome the top fears in the workplace so that they may be open to receiving your messages and act on your suggestions and ideas.

Helping others overcome their fears is critical in achieving breakthrough communication, whether we are in the position of a leader or a peer. Keys to this are open communication, transparency, and honesty, as well as a willingness to engage people on a human level. Also important are context and information where gaps exist, lest we let rumors and conjecture run rampant to create an atmosphere of uncertainty and fear.

The Upside of Fear

Just as fear can be paralyzing and stop us from fully participating in professional and personal opportunities, fear also helps us in myriad ways that the breakthrough communicator should be aware of.

Fear of embarrassment and repercussions is what makes us show up at meetings on time. Fear of punishment and fines has most of us pay our taxes on time, keep to the speed limit, and otherwise adhere to the many rules and customs our societies have created for an orderly life.

Fear of losing to the competition has us work harder in business, office politics, sports, and many other endeavors, from the professional to the personal.

Academy Award–winning actor and *Batman* star Christian Bale is quoted as saying, "I have a fear of being boring." Considering his impressive performances and diverse body of work, Bale's fear may just be his greatest motivator to deliver outstanding entertainment.

Smart communicators understand the benefits of healthy psychological fear and know when to harness it in others for mutual gain.

In the next chapter we'll examine how ambivalence in others can thwart our best communication efforts every bit as much as fear can. To manage ambivalence we look at nudging and other insights gleaned from behavioral economics that open the doors to our messages to spark desired actions.

CHAPTER 13

Managing Ambivalence

People are funny. We say we want to invest in our careers and do meaningful work, and we put off getting those extra credentials and remain in unsatisfying jobs. We celebrate Earth Day and proceed to let everybody know about it by printing and distributing a ton of paper flyers. We want to get in shape and eat a healthier diet, and we moan to our friends about our expanding waistlines over beer, burgers, and fries. We want both *this* and *not this* at the same time.

In our quest to spark action in our breakthrough communication process, we need to be aware that even when people have decided to change, they nonetheless may have stubborn underlying resistances to doing so. In the following pages, I've attempted to provide you with tools for compassionately helping people get in touch with their hidden ambivalences so as to draw those ambivalences into the open and quite possibly get beyond them.

Understand Others' Competing Priorities
(That Influence Their Behavior)

So how do you make sense of a colleague who says she's enthusiastic about your agenda, confirms that the meaning you give to the issues resonates, but never goes beyond that verbal support into active participation? You could write her off as flaky, inconsistent, or shallow, or you could try understand why she's waffling and thus move her off of the bench and onto your team of active supporters—the result of breakthrough communication.

We like to think of ourselves as levelheaded thinkers with all our arrows pointing in the same direction, but when faced with a novel choice or idea, even one entirely congruent with our own values and goals, we find ourselves wavering. Why? Because before that moment we might never have thought through the consequences of that choice, and now that the option is in front of us, we're not sure what it really means and if we really want it. It's easy to say you want to go skydiving someday, but when you're getting the parachute strapped on and you climb into the plane, you might just reconsider whether or not this is a good idea. In other words, you're *actively* conflicted about your priorities. The thrill and cachet of jumping out of a plane at 10,000 feet or the safety and comfort of two feet firmly on the ground?

We might also be *passively* conflicted. In these cases we don't necessarily recognize a conflict; instead, we put off making choices we know we should make. For example, most people would agree that saving for retirement is a sound and sensible thing to do, and the sooner one starts the better, but how many actually do so? At one work site, union officials made a point to talk to each union member about union benefits, including health insurance and a pension plan, and provided paperwork for those members as well as instructions on where to send it. Many members would follow through on the insurance paperwork, knowing they would likely need that benefit sooner rather than later, but they didn't apply for the pension benefit. Why not? Some couldn't imagine working there long enough for the benefit to pay off; others didn't want their contribution taken out of their paychecks or thought the pension wouldn't be worth much; and for still others, retirement was so far away as to not matter. Saving for retirement made *theoretical* sense, but as a day-to-day matter, it was easy to ignore.

To spark your waffling colleague into action, you first have to figure out the *source* of her indecision. Does she like you personally but is she wary about your agenda? Does she think you have good ideas but is she concerned about their workability? Does she want to support you but is she worried about the impact on her day-to-day job responsibilities? Does she feel caught in the middle between competing agendas offered by multiple colleagues? These are all forms of active conflict or ambivalence, which will require you to gather more information about her priorities in order to reassure her that your agenda does not compete with other perceived priorities, but rather it supports her own goals.

On the other hand, perhaps she hasn't acted because she doesn't know what, exactly, to do.

Let's say you're in charge of redesigning your company website in order to raise the organization's profile and reach a broader customer base, and you've asked for suggestions on those changes. She agrees to ponder improvements, but you never hear from her; when you ask the web administrator if your colleague has sent any suggestions his way, he shrugs and says no. You observe that she's meeting all her other responsibilities, but in this instance she has dropped off the radar. So what's going on? Your colleague may be very interested in being seen as a creative team player who enthusiastically contributes ideas to marketing projects but may feel that the current website already clearly represents the organizational message and brand image, and thus can't provide specific input. Not "getting it" or not knowing what to do may put her in a situation of stasis.

Dimensions of Resistance

When your allegedly supportive colleague doesn't follow through, it's easy to think that she's resisting you; that is, she's not really on board with your agenda. Sandy Kristin Piderit, writing in the

Academy of Management Review, noted that it is common for managers to characterize seemingly skeptical employees as short-sighted and resistant. More recently, however, social scientists have burrowed into the concept of *ambivalence,* dividing it into three dimensions: the emotional, the cognitive, and the intentional (regarding whether or not to support something new). When these dimensions are in conflict with one another or even if there is conflict within a single dimension ("on the one hand, but on the other hand"), ambivalence arises. Piderit observes that someone may react emotionally against change even as he agrees with the reasoning behind the change. She offers the example of a manager who was told, late in the planning cycle, that incentive money for distributors would no longer be available and instead assigned elsewhere. He was upset with the abruptness of the announcement and frustrated at its lateness; yet cognitively he agreed that the changes made sense. His ambivalence arose from a conflict between his emotional and cognitive states.

By conceiving of ambivalence in this trilevel manner, you can better pinpoint the source of your colleague's inaction. Let's say her issue of concern is your agenda. Given that she has been an ardent supporter of yours in the past and continues to respond positively to your suggestions, you could conclude that the problem is at neither the cognitive nor the intentional level; the problem might therefore be at the emotional level. In other words, while she thinks your ideas are good and would improve the company's prospects, she worries about what the implementation of your agenda ultimately means for her. Clearly, establishing your personal and professional credibility with her is key in soliciting her support, but when you want her to act on your behalf, you have to demonstrate that such action is congruent with her own priorities, thus neutralizing emotional resistance.

Emotional resistance can also stem from her perception that you consulted her too late in the process—she is in charge of customer service, after all, and as a stakeholder she knows the customers' needs, strengths, and vulnerabilities better than anyone else—and resents your attempts to leapfrog over her.

It's important to recognize and respond to that emotional ambivalence, lest it lead to increased skepticism about and less support for your agenda. Her initial positive response to you and your ideas might have been based on the understanding that possible negative consequences of the agenda would be affirmatively dealt with. The longer these possibilities go unaddressed, the greater the likelihood that you lose credibility with her; and as a result her cognitive and intentional support wanes. Understanding that ambivalence is multidimensional can also help you to manage flagging support after the initial burst of enthusiasm: your colleagues may accept your agenda but still become frustrated as you move to implement it. By staying on top of and encouraging the expression of their ambivalence, you can head off a turn into resistance and negativity.

Piderit notes that cognitive ambivalence is often most apparent because employees or colleagues are comfortable articulating their reasons for their skepticism. On the other hand, emotional ambivalence is more often expressed indirectly, for example, through humor. Piderit explains, "In such a case, more data about the change initiative might not be very useful. . . . Instead, more impromptu and casual conversations might be more effective in creating an atmosphere in which employees feel safe expressing their negative emotional responses openly." Cognitive ambivalence might also be best dealt with through listening, as "overselling the benefits of the change may not be effective in securing employee support, if employees already accept that the change will have some positive outcome but feel a different perspective is required."

Ambivalence can actually work in your favor if you use it to obtain feedback. Piderit speculates that "the honest expression of ambivalence seems more likely to generate dialogue than the expression of either determined opposition or firm support." She also cites scholars who suggest that ambivalence can open up discussions of the status quo, which in turn can motivate people to consider new approaches; even after your colleagues or employees state their agreement with your agenda, however, keep in mind that they might still feel ambivalent, such that ambivalence management is best seen as a process rather than a onetime event. In any case, recognizing both the existence and source(s) of ambivalence provides opportunities for discussion and refinement of your goals.

Structuring the Context for Better Choices

Whether ambivalence is active or passive—or emotional, cognitive, or intentional—sparking desired actions in ambivalent souls requires powerful tools.

One such set of tools is embedded in the term *choice architecture*, conceived by economist Richard Thaler and law professor Cass Sunstein and made popular in their book *Nudge* (2009).

Not unlike the concepts we are discussing in this book, where the issues we make salient and agendas we establish and meanings we infuse influence the decisions and reactions of others, nudging also targets choices. The authors of *Nudge* assert that myriad choices can be presented in such a way that decision makers select one option over the other without having their freedom of choice restricted. We are simply being nudged in the "right" direction.

The realization that we face thousands of choices on a daily basis, from the mundane—Dunkin' Donuts coffee or Starbucks on the way to work?—to the profound—take the promotion or go back to school?—is enlightening, to say the least. It is a sobering reminder that we need to work harder to get people's attention, to more astutely appeal to their rational and irrational hopes and fears and values and beliefs that guide all decision making.

Just as our struggle to determine the agenda and spin meaning defines outcomes, so does the development of choices and arrangement of context, as in choice architecture.

It's less complicated than it sounds, and examples in literature and the real world abound. In fact, Chapter 1 of my last book, *360 Degrees of Influence*, starts with just such examples:

> A New Zealand bank helpfully nudges customers to save money on impulse by just pressing a button on their iPhone. Apparently there is an app for that. School cafeterias across the United States are experimenting with the presentation of healthier food choices—making fruit and vegetables more appealing than the more popular fried food by improving their lighting, positioning, and names (carrots called "X-ray veggies," anyone?). New York taxicabs have a touchscreen on the back of the front seat suggesting how much passengers should tip the driver upon arriving at a destination. Big, colorful buttons give the option of paying $2, $3, or $4 if the fare is less than $15. If your fare is more than $15, the buttons display percentages from 20 to 25 to 30 percent. Clearly counting on people's laziness or inability to calculate and self-select a fair tip, cabbies are happy to report that gratuities have shot way up, again due in part to these highly suggestive buttons that are tilted toward generosity.

Some other ways that simple changes in structure and context alter people's behavior include feedback, collaboration, and transparency. For example:

○ Telling people you welcome their feedback is great for a climate of open communication and transparency. But keeping your office door closed during business hours is sending the opposite signal. Therefore, take your "open-door policy" from the metaphorical to the literal and keep the door open.

○ Collaboration among teams and individuals of diverse backgrounds and areas of expertise is a key to success in many organizations, large and small. While people may be convinced of the need and be quite open to participating in these sessions, cramped office quarters, sterile meeting rooms with shrill lighting, and bad seating make the default choice of sitting at one's desk less of a pain. Creating more inspiring meeting facilities, even off-site, with multimedia access and other brainstorming resources can nudge people to get together on their own rather than by mandate only.

○ Leaders who want to hear what people really think and want to open up discussions about pressing issues may want to forgo their formal presentations and meetings environment, with the presenter up front, in favor of more informally arranged town hall–style meetings. Participants typically feel freer to voice their opinions and ask questions of their colleagues and managers in these contexts.

Let's also look at the classic corporate presentation as an example of choice architecture. Most readers will have given one or two in their career. Audience members have choices: they can pay attention to you, daydream about the weekend, or answer e-mails on their iPhones while you present. If you, however, demonstrate that you "get them"—if you offer them a clear value up front, make your presentation easy to follow with lots of interesting insights applicable to your audience members' lives, loaded with emotional content via stories that resonate, all the while engaging them on a human level via dialogue—you are structuring the environment in such a way that the audience *chooses* to stay with you and learn from you, as opposed to tuning you out from the start. And if post-presentation you want your listeners to glean important details from your collateral materials and handouts, you'll have to make sure your materials are easy to read, logically structured, attractively designed, and available at just the right moment.

Let's explore a couple of other reasons people hold off committing to an action. Thaler and his colleagues note that bad design can lead to confusion, as when a door you expect to pull to open instead requires a push: even pasting a large sign above the handle saying PUSH is unlikely to be enough to overcome the urge to pull. And who hasn't had the experience of landing on a website looking for, say, product information and having to click and click and click to find a particular product—and then the specs aren't listed! What are the chances you've continued clicking versus quickly moving to the next website in frustration? As a breakthrough communicator, you don't want to handicap your listeners' ability to participate in your agenda: you want to *enable* them!

Scholar Eric Johnson and his colleagues laid out some additional obstacles to choice and identified how to overcome them through a variety of choice architecture tactics. One problem they list is "alternative overload," or too many choices. From brands of mustard and wine to cable channels and auto insurance providers, the number of options available makes one's head spin. And head spinning is not good if you want people to take action. While a mustard brand's choice architecture involves strategic location of shelf space at eye level—provided the brand has the clout and deep pockets required—in our context it may mean cutting down the number of alternatives.

Rather than tasking someone with finding "a new web designer," limit the options to, say, finding someone local who can meet face-to-face, someone with expertise in developing mobile apps, or someone with at least 10 years of relevant database experience. Similarly, in trying to spark action for a proposal the decision makers have bought into, limit the number of options you offer to actually taking the first step. Rather than "We can start today, tomorrow, or anytime," encourage the stakeholders to start on a specific date or specify any other relevant milestone.

Deadlines paired with staging can be especially effective in sparking action in colleagues. Perhaps the implementation of your agenda requires a long rollout period, such that your colleagues' involvement is required only at certain stages. Johnson and his colleagues recommend what they call "decision staging," that is, breaking down the process into discrete stages. In this way you could tell a team member whose support you need, "I'll need your participation at stages 1 through 3 and then not again until the sixth stage." In doing so you limit her responsibilities to, say, those in which she has some expertise. Adding specific dates to those stage rollouts also gives her the information she needs to arrange her own priorities.

Choice architecture as it's been developed is itself dependent on the notion that people are not, contra some economic theories, wholly rational. Amos Tversky and Daniel Kahneman pioneered studies on what are now commonly referred to as "cognitive biases," that is, oft-unconscious preferences for one option over another. The "endowment effect" is a common cognitive bias: people in general would rather hang on to what they have than trade it for something of equal or even greater value. This is not unrelated to the status quo bias, in which people would rather stick with what they know than risk the unknown; both involve loss aversion, or the worry that they'll be worse off after any change.

Say you'd like a colleague to participate on an innovation project that would benefit from his many years of expertise in his position. He understands the challenges and can meet them due to his experience and know-how. And yet he's ambivalent in his commitment to action. The innovative changes you proposed, and for which you have stakeholder buy-in, may threaten the status quo that your expert has contributed to and has a stake in keeping, lest his expertise is no longer of equal value in the new environment in spite of evidence to the contrary. Openly, however, this subject-matter expert continues to express his support; after all, who wants to be perceived to be standing in the way of innovation and progress?

By understanding this bias and recognizing his ambivalence, you have the opportunity to assuage the expert's fears of losing status, emphasize his current value to the project, and communicate a compelling vision of the future that allows him to see his place in it clearly and, if applicable, with increasing value and responsibility.

In order to succeed as choice architect, it's imperative that you understand the biases and competing priorities you're dealing with in the environment you construct. Johnson and his colleagues quote learning theorist Hobart Mowrer: "To understand or predict what a rat will learn to do in a maze, one has to know both the rat and the maze." I hope you don't think of your colleagues as rats, but to piggyback on Mowrer's analogy, when you think of how your colleagues respond to uncertainty or challenge, you'll likely want to consider that while Todd likes to race through a problem, Chris prefers to mull over every available option, and Lourdes will ask lots of questions before proceeding. Armed with this information about each of the stakeholders, you can construct choices in ways that appeal to each member's decision-making process.

Choice architecture, in other words, is really about structuring incentives, be they aimed toward our emotions, our thoughts, or our unconscious biases, so that we are driven to act. Given all the work you've done to get yourself on the radar, establish salience in setting the agenda, and infuse that agenda with meaning, it only makes sense to use the tools and insights of choice architecture to increase your odds of sparking action and creating breakthroughs.

In the next and final chapter we discuss how learning from important feedback can make us even more effective in our efforts at breakthrough communication as we learn from examples of leaders throughout history who turned failure into success to come out ahead in the end.

CHAPTER 14

Learning from Feedback: It's Not Over 'til It's Over

Even with everything we've learned, maybe the end of the process is not quite as you had wished. You did everything as you were "supposed to" in the breakthrough communication process, and now here you are at the "spark"—but it isn't your desired outcome. Maybe you got on the radar of that decision maker at the Fortune 100 company for a plum position in management, and you've successfully set the agenda and clearly communicated your meaning. Yet your efforts didn't result in the outcome you had your sights on. Rather than offering you a full-time job, complete with benefits and bonus package, you were offered a short-term consulting gig at the firm. What do you do?

There can definitely be a tendency to retreat in disgust, to wallow in self-pity or defeat, or to blame yourself, your audience, or the process. Don't! The connection you made is your spark, even if it doesn't go as you initially planned. It is an opportunity to continue to engage in a communication process and move toward your goals. It's possible, as the saying goes, that one door has shut but a window has opened. You have an incredibly valuable chance to learn from this new outcome and to continue to shape how you would like the situation to continue. As I've talked about before, it's important to see your audience's side of the story. What are your listeners saying or offering, and how can you link that to your original goals and plans? Did you miss something? Are you, in fact, being given a chance to revise and start again or perhaps to jump back to an earlier step in the process?

In this chapter, we'll explore listening to feedback and learning from it. Human history—as well as literary works that draw inspiration from real-life human experience—is replete with examples of people who have overcome setbacks, learned from an initial poor outcome, and gone on to notable success. Human history is also full of people who *should* have done so. So why didn't they? It can be easy to retreat when we don't get what we want, and it can be tempting to shut down or give in to fear. But when we understand feedback as a chance to reexamine our approach and our process, we can view it not as a failure but as a new avenue toward success.

To Listen or Not to Listen?

Let's begin with two examples from literature that demonstrate how people *didn't* listen to feedback. Shakespeare is, again, a great teacher here, as his plays are brimming with characters and situations spawned from poor communication. For example, *Romeo and Juliet*—great story, but a terrible outcome. The characters are fun to read about or watch, but you sure wouldn't want to be them! How did these two young, passionate lovers go so wrong as to both end up dead? Was their mistake falling in love? Hardly! Their mistake was in *thinking small* and not trusting their ability to *strike out in a new direction*. At the start of the play, there is a fierce feud between their families, the Montagues and Capulets. When Romeo falls in love with Juliet and then gets in a fatal brawl with Juliet's cousin Tybalt, the situation goes from bad to worse, and Romeo is banished from the city. How do the characters respond? Do they, like many of us might, decide to leave their bad situation behind them and start again somewhere new, seeing Romeo's banishment as an opportunity? Unfortunately, no. Romeo cannot imagine a life outside Verona, so instead of changing his plans, he panics and decides to put his and Juliet's fates in the hands of an idealistic, social-engineering friar who proposes to reconcile their families by giving Juliet a sleeping potion to make everyone think she is dead. Sad to say, everything doesn't go according to plan, and the entire situation ends in tragedy.

What was the action Romeo wanted to spark? He wanted to be able to live happily with Juliet. He was certainly on the radar of Juliet and her family, albeit as a sworn enemy. But rather than setting the agenda—that he wished to marry Juliet—he continued to operate under the framework of animosity presented to him. He saw Juliet in secret, and he responded to the violence and poor communication with more violence and lack of communication. As the situation grew increasingly worse, Romeo did not take the opportunity to examine the present and find a new way to communicate—he simply continued along the same path. Romeo could have changed the minds of the feuding families by clearly communicating his meaning and desires, by showing how happy he and Juliet were, or by explaining Juliet's dislike for her arranged husband, Paris. He and Juliet could have made a plan together. But the two star-crossed lovers saw anything short of their desired outcome as negative feedback and complete failure. They were unable to even adequately communicate with each other: Juliet planned to fake her own death and did so before Romeo could find out. Upon seeing her dead and Paris in her crypt, Romeo simply continued to charge ahead the way he always had, killing himself moments before Juliet awoke from her sleep. Both she and Romeo refused to be flexible, communicate, or critically assess the feedback they received, and their stories ended in tragedy because of it.

We can see a similar example in *King Lear*, another of Shakespeare's tragedies. The stubborn king just cannot learn from his mistakes. In a fit of annoyance he banishes the only daughter who truly loves him, and he puts himself in the hands of his two other daughters. Then he banishes his only truly loyal nobleman for pointing out his mistake. When the first of the evil daughters shows her true colors, Lear cannot back up and meet with his loyal daughter. He is too ashamed to admit his mistake, so he turns to the second evil daughter. It's been said that the definition of insanity is doing the same thing over and over expecting different results, and we can certainly see that with King Lear. Because he was caught up in fear and set in his old ways, he persisted until he came to an untimely end.

Of course, these stories are tragedies, so the characters in a sense had to behave as they did. Later in this chapter, we will explore some positive real-life examples of people who *did* learn from feedback and tried something new. But for now, let's turn back to what we've learned from the breakthrough communication process so far to identify useful tools for dealing with feedback.

Time to Reflect

We've covered the four steps of the process—radar, agenda, meaning, and spark—and we know that one of the useful features of this step-by-step structure is that we can look at each step in turn to see where we may have gone wrong. In the example that opened this chapter—being offered a consulting assignment instead of a full-time position—you can ask yourself useful questions about how you employed breakthrough communication. Did you clearly tap into the present moment—did you adequately explain why you felt this particular company needs you on board full-time *right now*? Did you draw on all the tools at your disposal? Maybe your narrative didn't resonate with the members of your audience as it should have. Try to imagine things from their point of view. Perhaps they really want to hire you on full-time but don't have the funds available. If they tell you this, listen to their concerns and try to imagine yourself in their position—what would you do? Explain how you can be valuable, and then, rather than letting the outcome of a temporary engagement "just happen" to you, put your skills to use. Now that you're on their radar, find ways to use your new status and the new information you have as part of their company to try to improve the company's earnings and demonstrate your value. Be flexible and restart the process from the beginning, drawing on the new tools at your disposal to accomplish your goals. They're likely to see it your way soon.

Of course, this doesn't mean that everything you do is simply a way to get what you initially wanted. It's important to remain open to new opportunities. As with the example of *Romeo and Juliet*, the characters remained too fixated on their initial goals to recognize new opportunities. In our job example, perhaps you accept the consultant offer. Then as you get a feel for the company, you see that a full-time position or one at that particular company isn't right for you after all. If you had turned down the offer, you wouldn't have known that, and you might have been consumed with regret or negative feelings. Remember that this feedback is an *opportunity* to assess, reconsider, learn, and grow.

The Comeback Kids

Let's turn to a few examples of real-life people who learned and grew from opportunities.

Napoleon Bonaparte is one such example. When he was exiled to Elba in 1814, he was initially so devastated that he attempted suicide. He didn't succeed, however, and he soon managed to turn the tables on the rest of Europe. Seeing that the French people despised King Louis and recognizing that the time was right for his return, Napoleon eventually staged a daring escape under the noses of his captors. When troops were sent to intercept him, he *talked them into joining his cause* instead—a case of breakthrough communication if there ever was one! He dismounted his horse and approached the troops, declaring "Here I am! Kill your Emperor, if you wish!" Soon he was leading a force of 200,000 soldiers, and he came very close to victory in the final battle against the forces that had exiled him. How did this happen?

In his bold statement to his potential captors, Napoleon risked everything. He could have been shot on sight, and all his plans could have gone to waste. But when he staged his escape, he knew the political tide was changing. If we look at the situation through the lens of breakthrough communication, Napoleon was obviously on the troops' radar as a fugitive from justice. But instead of accepting this, Napoleon set the agenda himself. He approached the troops rather than running away or turning himself over. He exuded confidence by not showing fear. He created salience, deciding what was important by announcing himself as "your Emperor," setting the stage for the troops' change of heart. He found common ground with them because he continued to follow France's political situation and knew that the time was right for his return. While he was ultimately unsuccessful, this powerful change never could have happened if he had succeeded in his suicide attempt or had admitted defeat. Napoleon remained focused on his goals, even in exile, and waited for a new opportunity to go after them. He even used the initial setback of his exile to his advantage, knowing that a dramatic return and attempt to overthrow the current regime would be all the more powerful because of the narrative of his exile. The dramatic story of the troops' change of heart must have won many more followers to his cause than he could have any other way.

You may not be facing down troops on horseback, but you may well have setbacks you can turn into opportunities. To turn to a more modern example, let's look at Steve Jobs, easily one of the most successful entrepreneurs in America. Jobs was fired from

Apple over disagreements with other members of the company. In his 2005 commencement speech at Stanford, Jobs reflected on the experience and said:

> So at 30 I was out [fired from Apple]. And very publicly out. What had been the focus of my entire adult life was gone, and it was devastating. I really didn't know what to do for a few months. I felt that I had let the previous generation of entrepreneurs down—that I had dropped the baton as it was being passed to me. I . . . tried to apologize for screwing up so badly. I was a very public failure, and I even thought about running away from the valley.

Being fired, feeling publically disgraced, and not knowing what to do next certainly didn't create the spark Jobs hoped for when he began the company! Like Napoleon, Jobs initially floundered in despair. But eventually his perspective changed:

> But something slowly began to dawn on me—I still loved what I did. The turn of events at Apple had not changed that one bit. I had been rejected, but I was still in love. And so I decided to start over. I didn't see it then, but it turned out that getting fired from Apple was the best thing that could have ever happened to me. The heaviness of being successful was replaced by the lightness of being a beginner again, less sure about everything. It freed me to enter one of the most creative periods of my life.

Jobs ultimately went on to found a company called NeXT. Many years later, Apple purchased NeXT, and Jobs found himself back at Apple. In his Stanford commencement speech, he said, "I'm pretty sure none of this would have happened if I hadn't been fired from Apple. It was awful-tasting medicine, but I guess the patient needed it."

Despite setbacks, Steve Jobs never lost sight of what he loved and never relinquished ownership of his dreams. After being fired from Apple, he could have withdrawn from the technology world, thinking he had no place in it. Instead, he continued to follow his passion, using his firing as an opportunity to become more flexible, productive, and creative. While it may look like getting rehired by Apple "just happened," it only happened because Jobs refused to let a negative situation change his goals. After a rocky period, he got back on Apple's radar with his talent, passion, and skills, and ultimately he rejoined the company as an even more valuable player because of the other experiences he had under his belt.

One powerful quality that we can take from this example is that, in a way, Jobs didn't let the experience of being fired become who he was; instead, he used the experience to reinvent himself. In his commencement address, he said that he felt like a public failure who had let down previous generations. He certainly saw himself this way, and maybe others did as well. But he didn't let that image stick for long. He set the agenda by getting back on his feet and coming out with a new company. When we don't get an outcome we want, it can be easy to label ourselves failures or undeserving, but by seeing every outcome as an opportunity, we can use these opportunities to our advantage.

Politics is full of examples of motivated, goal-oriented people making comebacks. Think of Abraham Lincoln: when you first hear his name, what do you think of? One of the most important presidents in American history? A man who changed the history of America for good? What you might *not* think of is a one-term congressman whose term ended in failure and ridicule. When he was a congressman, Lincoln stood in ardent opposition to then-president James K. Polk, especially against Polk's desire to declare war on Mexico. When President Polk attempted to justify the war by claiming that Mexican soldiers had "invaded *our territory* and shed the blood of our fellow-citizens on our *own soil*," Lincoln became so incensed that he demanded Polk provide Congress with the exact spots on which this blood had been shed to prove it was American. These were known as "Spot Resolutions," and Lincoln was so vocal about them that some people referred to him as "Spotty Lincoln." Congress ignored these resolutions, which resulted in a loss of popularity and political support for Lincoln. Lincoln later regretted his attacks on Polk and the reputation it garnered him. Much like Steve Jobs, Lincoln left Congress ashamed after one term and returned to practicing law in Illinois. This experience brought him into the ongoing debates about slavery, and he ultimately reentered politics to fight against the spread of slavery. He delivered many passionate and eloquent speeches that are still known today, all on his way to the White House—and all this from the man known as Spotty Lincoln!

In his pursuit of a career in politics, Lincoln was certainly on people's radar, but not in the way he wanted. When he left Congress, he didn't see his situation as a failure, but instead as an opportunity. He returned to the radar as an eloquent speaker with an agenda: stopping the spread of slavery. Slavery was a divisive subject at the time, but Lincoln's speeches spoke to common values held by his listeners. He spoke of the unity of the nation, the Constitution, and the intents of the founding fathers when they said that "all men are created equal" and have the right to "life, liberty, and the pursuit of happiness." In his famous "A House Divided" speech, he drew on the strong metaphor of the Union as a house and wove a powerful narrative, skills we've discussed in previous chapters. Through all this, he created a strong image of himself as a powerful and well-spoken antislavery politician. This image catapulted him into the White House and into the annals of history. He used leaving Congress as an opportunity to reinvent himself and pursue his goals from a different direction. The single-mindedness that caused him shame over his conflicts with President Polk brought him great success when framed in a new light.

During this same time period, Ulysses S. Grant also saw the particular political situation as a chance to reinvent himself. Though he had proved himself a valuable and skilled soldier during the Mexican-American War, he was kicked out of the army for excessive drinking. He floundered for several years in farming and selling leather goods. He built a house for his wife and family, which he considered an incredible achievement, but his wife hated it. So he went from being a highly commended soldier to being dismissed from the military to being unable to please his own wife—it didn't seem like life could get any worse. While the outbreak of the Civil War was arguably not a good thing, it was the opportunity Grant needed to get back into the military and become one of the most renowned Civil War generals and to ultimately become president of the United States.

In these examples, we see how Lincoln and Grant both faced setbacks that they overcame. When things did not go their way, they took control and changed the conversation. Both knew what they wanted and what they were good at; and when they didn't get their desired outcome right away, they took a step back, regrouped, and more or less completely reinvented themselves. Just as with Steve Jobs, in a way, their setbacks were the best things that could have happened to them. Not getting what they wanted right away provided the opportunity to reassess and to try a new tactic, angle, and image.

If you are in a similar situation in your own life, think about the ways in which your current outcome can be turned to your advantage. Maybe you need to set a new agenda, or maybe you need to take your current agenda to a new radar. Lincoln was not successful when he campaigned against Polk, but when he set his sights on slavery, everyone listened. Do you need to do the same? Failing to receive your desired outcome may be a sign that some part of your process is amiss, and you may need to start again from scratch. See it as an opportunity! You can use what you've learned from one situation to reinvent yourself in another, one that is more aligned with your goals.

Of course, history is full of successful people who did not completely reinvent themselves but succeeded anyway. One such example is George W. Bush. Like Grant, he had a drinking problem, and he had even been convicted of a drunk-driving incident. In 1978, he lost a congressional election when his opponent successfully cast him as out of touch with regular Texans. This was a major political lesson for Bush, who went on to become governor of Texas and later president. Though his career has been marked by controversy, he remained steadfast in his goals and values.

On the other side of the political spectrum is Bill Clinton, who acquired the nickname the "Comeback Kid" for rewinning the governorship of Arkansas in 1982, initially having lost the position in 1980 after serving a single term. He has since lived up to that nickname by regaining a large degree of political popularity in spite of having been impeached during his presidency. He is well remembered for his improvements to the economy, and he continues to work tirelessly for humanitarian causes to this day.

Bill Clinton's wife, Hillary Clinton, has had a similar experience to her husband's. Her years as First Lady were polarizing for the American people, especially in regard to her efforts to spearhead healthcare reform. Her husband's impeachment scandal cast speculation on her as well, but she managed to take control of the conversation in such a way that, during the scandal, her public approval ratings were at their peak. As a senator, she spoke out against the Bush administration's conduct in Iraq, and later she ran in the Democratic primaries for president. Though she lost to Barack Obama, she turned this setback into a success by becoming secretary of state, where she worked for the rights of women around the globe. (Obama himself was no stranger to setback: though he lost a Democratic primary race for Illinois's First Congressional District in the U.S. House of Representatives to four-term incumbent Bobby Rush by a margin of two to one, he went on from this defeat to win a Senate seat and ultimately the presidency.)

George W. Bush, Bill Clinton, and Hillary Clinton did not reinvent themselves in the way Lincoln and Grant did, but instead they took control of the controversy around them. All three of them had to rethink their relationships and political identities to line up better with the values of others. They incorporated their past mistakes into the narrative they were telling in order to take control of the situation. If you can't or don't want to reinvent yourself, try to see the ways that the feedback you're receiving can help you, or look for how you can spin an initially unfavorable outcome into a new, positive light. Clinton became the Comeback Kid by not seeing his first political loss and his impeachment as setbacks, but rather by drawing on them to reframe himself as someone who was resilient and able to overcome obstacles. George W. Bush, similarly, responded to his opponent's accusations that he was "out of touch" to make positive changes for the lives of Texans in improving education and in reducing the drug and crime rates, showing that he had people's interests in mind. Though his presidency was controversial, he was liked by many voters because he drew on these controversies to show how his goals were aligned with those of common people. Hillary Clinton used her husband's scandal to her advantage by framing herself as dedicated to her family and to the rights of women, images that gained her popular support and helped her earn her position as secretary of state.

These three set their own agenda and made meaning by taking control of the feedback they received. Perhaps you can do the same in your own situation. In our previous example of being offered a temporary position when you wanted a full-time one, could you incorporate that offer into a narrative of yourself as a free agent or as someone able to bring about a large amount of change in a short period of time? Such an image could potentially be leveraged into a full-time position, or it could get you noticed on others' radars and open up new opportunities you never even dreamed of.

Lest you think the only examples are from politics, the world of entertainment also furnishes many examples of people who were not deterred or sidelined by early negative reviews. Elvis Presley, for instance, initially received negative reviews from the press and during live performances. Legend has it that after his first (and last) live performance at the Grand Ole Opry, he was advised by the Opry's talent coordinator to go back to driving trucks. Nevertheless, he went on to become one of the most famous musicians of all time.

Similarly, the Beatles did not fare well in their first audition for a recording contract. Decca Records rejected the Beatles, saying "guitar groups are on the way out." We all know how that turned out!

Elvis and the Beatles are both examples of people who didn't take no for an answer. They knew they had something that people wanted, and the musical and personal styles of both groups were something that strongly resonated with young audiences at the time. The people who rejected them were from the "old" generation, in many ways still stuck in the past and set in their ideas of what music should be and what people should want. Elvis and the Beatles did something new, and while it may initially have been frightening or controversial, they ultimately found the right audience and went on to be big successes. What can you learn from these examples? In both cases, it seems like these entertainers were initially on the wrong radar; they had the ears of the wrong people, people who wouldn't be able to connect with their story or align with their goals. They could have taken the rejections of these initial audiences to heart and given up, but they didn't; instead, they found new audiences and people they could really connect with. Perhaps your own setbacks are a sign that you are talking to the wrong people or are on the wrong radar. If you have an idea that you know is great, take it to others who will support you, even if they aren't the people you may initially have thought of. Think carefully about who might value what you have to offer and why. Elvis and the Beatles knew that young people would love their music, and that's who they eventually took it to. When music industry executives saw the public's reaction, they knew they had to get on board.

Though all the examples we've seen in this chapter are very different, what they all have in common is that the individuals involved overcame adversity and setbacks in order to go on to success. Unlike Romeo, Juliet, and King Lear, these success stories were able to be flexible in the face of disappointment. They used seeming rejections as chances to reinvent themselves, and they incorporated feedback that didn't align with their story into their narrative in order to grow stronger and more relatable. Each step of the breakthrough communication process provides a clear chance to revise, realign, and try again. We can take control of the outcome with the tools we've learned so far; we can learn to search for creative solutions and new tipping points to get at our desired spark. Breakthrough communication is cyclical, and this particular spark is just one step in an ongoing process.

NOTES

Chapter 1: The Art of Getting on the Radar

I was reminded of this on a day I presented: Harrison Monarth, personal communication.

"If you're looking for an opportunity": http://www.linkedin.com/today /post/article/20130130215042-1213-connect-to-human-networks-to -find-breakout-opportunities.

Two years ago, a team of psychologists, from Canada, Belgium, and the United States: http://www.sciencedaily.com/releases/2011/01 /110118113445.htm.

"Our findings suggest there are really two ways to top the social ladder and gain leadership": http://www.publicaffairs.ubc.ca/2012/12/19/for-power -and-status-dominance-and-skill-trump-likability/.

In a piece for the Harvard Business Review, Bryan Garner offers: http:// blogs.hbr.org/2013/02/write-e-mails-that-people-wont/.

Professor V. Bhaskar, from University College London: http://www.ucl.ac .uk/~uctpvbh/beauty-final.pdf.

A study entitled "Feminine Charm: An Experimental Analysis of Its Costs and Benefits in Negotiations": http://www.haas.berkeley.edu/groups /online_marketing/facultyCV/papers/kray_paper2012.pdf.

Tom Peters revolutionized this concept back in 1997: http://www .fastcompany.com/28905/brand-called-you.

At Columbia's Graduate School of Journalism, Sree Sreenivasan, dean of student affairs: http://www.nytimes.com/2012/03/01/education/digital -skills-can-be-quickly-acquired.html?pagewanted=all&_r=0.

Take Havard Rugland, a 28-year-old from a small town in Norway: http:// www.nytimes.com/2012/12/29/sports/football/norwegian-earns -internet-stardom-and-an-nfl-tryout-to-boot.html?pagewanted=all.

Chapter 2: Managing Your Status

NYU's Stern School of Business professor Steven Blader and Cornell University professor Ya-Ru Chen wrote an article: http://psycnet.apa.org/psycinfo/2012-00031-001/.

People are like dogs: http://pages.uoregon.edu/sanjay/pubs/poweraccuracy.pdf.

People who are extraverted and/or physically attractive are more likely: John Anderson, Keltner, and Kring, 2001. http://www.ncbi.nlm.nih.gov/pubmed/11474718

"and individuals with dominant personalities can often be singled out from a postage-stamp sized avatar because they tend to have distinct facial features": http://mors.haas.berkeley.edu/research/anderson/accurate%20when%20it%20counts.pdf

A widely used tool in the corporate world: http://edweb.sdsu.edu/people/arossett/pie/Interventions/360_1.htm.

Fast, assistant professor of management and organization at the University of Southern California's Marshall School of Business: http://www.stanford.edu/group/knowledgebase/cgi-bin/2011/09/20/power-corrupts-especially-when-it-lacks-status/.

I'm reminded of a situation I observed at my hotel while on a recent trip to Singapore: Harrison Monarth, personal communication.

Barbara Kellerman, the James MacGregor Burns Lecturer in Public Leadership: http://blogs.hbr.org/2008/06/clinton-is-no-role-model-for-w/.

Chapter 3: Finding Common Ground

Houdini was born Erich Weisz in Budapest: William Kalish and Larry Sloman, *The Secret Life of Harry Houdini: The Making of America's First Superhero* (New York: Atria, 2006).

He soon became the first performer with a "dumb act": Joe Laurie Jr., *Vaudeville: From the Honky-Tonks to the Palace* (New York: Henry Holt & Co., 1953).

Fogle's story began when he was just a 20-year-old junior at Indiana University: http://adage.com/article/news/subway-stop-jonesing-jared/125142/.

In 2008, Subway was the second most recognizable brand behind Burger King: http://adage.com/article/news/subway-stop-jonesing-jared/125142/.

As Thomas Leeper, PhD, writes in "Polarized": http://www.psychologytoday.com/blog/polarized/201211/finding-common-ground-in-divisive-times-0.

In an interview on NPR's Talk of the Nation, Foley explained it this way: http://www.npr.org/2012/07/12/156677236/finding-common-ground -in-environmental-debates.

A 2011 study from the University of Notre Dame: http://magazine.nd.edu /news/40683-having-coffee-with-tim-judge/.

Chapter 5: Setting the Agenda: Focusing on What Really Matters

Basically any time someone opens his or her mouth: This understanding of salience-agenda owes a great deal to Richard E. Vatz's concept as discussed in *The Only Authentic Book of Persuasion*, 2nd ed. (Dubuque, IA: Kendall Hunt Publishing Co., 2012). As he notes on p. 7, "Virtually every communication is an effort to create issue salience or attention of the chosen audience." He later observes persuaders "strategically promote saliences and meanings for chosen audiences, and, when successful, these pass for real conditions to which it seems we must pay attention" (p. 32).

Political scientist Thomas Birkland defines: Thomas Birkland, "Focusing Events, Mobilization, and Agenda Setting," *Journal of Public Policy* 18 no. 1 (1998): 54.

He notes that "Focusing events": Ibid., 55.

Common types of focusing events in politics: Saundra K. Schneider, "Lessons of Disaster: Policy Change After Catastropic Events," *Journal of Public Administration Research & Theory* 19 (2009): 989–995. See also Don Wolfensburger, "From Sputnik to the Moon: How Focusing Events Transformed American Government," Congress Project Seminar, Woodrow Wilson International Center for Scholars, May 14, 2007.

Advocacy groups who are dissatisfied: Birkland, op. cit., 55; see also Claire B. Rubin, Imak Renda Tanali, and William R. Cumming, "Disaster Time Line: Focusing Events and U.S. Outcomes (1969–2004)." http:// www.gwu.edu/~icdrm/publications/DTL04Jan28.pdf

They're not always successful: See Jan Váně, František Kalvas, "Focusing Events and Their Effect on Agenda-Setting," Paper prepared for the WAPOR Conference, Hong Kong, 2012, and Schneider, op. cit.

Malcolm Gladwell has famously: Malcolm Gladwell, *Tipping Point* (Boston: Little, Brown and Company, 2000), 9.

Maxwell McCombs and Donald Shaw, in their classic 1972 article: Malcolm E. McCombs and Donald L. Shaw, "The Agenda-Setting Function of Mass Media," *The Public Opinion Quarterly* 36, no. 2 (Summer 1972): 176–187.

Chris Vargo is among those attempting: Chris J. Vargo, "Twitter as Public Salience: An Agenda-Setting Effects Analysis," Moeller Student Paper Competition Entry, n.d. See also Chris W. Bonneau et. al., "Agenda Control, The Median Justice, and the Majority Opinion on the Supreme Court," *American Journal of Political Science* 51, no. 4 (October 2007): 890–905; Marilyn Roberts, Wayne Wanta, Tzong Horng (Dustin) Dzwo, "Agenda-Setting and Issue Salience Online," *Communication Research* 29 , no. 4 (August 2002): 452–465; and Michael B. Salwen, "Effect of a Cumulation of Coverage on Issue Salience in Agenda Setting," *Journalism Quarterly* 65 (1995): 100–106, 130.

Psychologist Laura Belsten: Laura Belsten, Institute for Social + Emotional Intelligence.

Chapter 6: Clarifying Focus and Objective

Ron Ashkenas, managing partner of Schaffer Consulting: Ron Ashkenas, "The Key to Effectiveness? Focus," *Harvard Business Review Blog Network*, September 1, 2009.

THIS, Inc. CEO Greg McKeown notes: Greg McKeown, "The Disciplined Pursuit of Less," *Harvard Business Review Blog Network*, August 8, 2012.

Business consultant Dr. Timothy Bednarz advises: Timothy Bednarz, "Objectives Allow Managers to Focus on Obtaining Results," *Leaders to Leader*, Majorium Business Press, 2013. http://blog.majorium businesspress.com/2013/02/04/objectives-allow-managers-to-focus-on -obtaining-results/

One lobbyist for a trade association in London: "London Girl," as quoted in Hannah Morton-Hedges, "What's It Like Working as a Political Lobbyist?" *Career Geek*, January 28, 2012. See also "Career: Lobbyist," *The Princeton Review*, 2013.

American League of Lobbyists president Paul Miller echoes: Paul Miller, as quoted in Jeanne Sahadi, "Six-Figure Jobs: Lobbying," *CNNMoney*, January 27, 2005.

Greg McKeown, who noted that the opportunities: McKeown, op. cit.

We'll take our inspiration from the philosopher: Arnold Schopenaur, as listed in "Quotes About Clarity," goodreads.com.

Doctor Noni MacDonald and reporter André Picard: Noni MacDonald and André Picard, "A Plea for Clear Language on Vaccine Safety," *Canadian Medical Association Journal* 180, no. 7 (March 31, 2009): 697–698.

Among the causes of this ignorance is the unclear meaning: Paula Yohe, "Getting Literacy Information Standards Noticed," *Library Media Connection* 28–30 (November/December 2007).

Instead, follow the advice which one journalism professor: Terri Peterson, personal communication.

That professor apparently followed the line laid down: George Orwell, "Politics and the English Language," originally published in *Horizon*, April 1946.

Similarly, the late scholar Tony Judt cautioned: Tony Judt, as quoted in Matt Cardin, "On Clarity of Language, Thought, Consciousness, and Being," *The Teeming Mind*, July 30, 2010.

He gives the example of a psychiatrist: Gerd Gigerenzer, *Calculated Risks* (New York: Simon & Schuster, 2002), 4–5.

Gigerenzer traces these and other problems: Ibid., 24.

One colleague—a college professor—takes care in her classroom: Terri Peterson, personal communication.

Adam Gopnik offers a cautionary tale: Adam Gopnik, "LOL," *The Moth*, December 13, 2006.

Chapter 7: Making New Ideas Salient

Addams was born in 1860 in Cedarville: Information in this section was taken from Bruce S. Jansson, *The Reluctant Welfare State*, 6th ed. (Belmont, CA: Brooks Cole, 2009); "Jane Addams—Biographical," The Nobelprize.org, Nobel Media AB 2013; and Lawrence Shulman, *The Skills of Helping Individuals, Families, Groups, and Communities*, 4th ed. (Itasca, IL: F. E. Peacock, 1999).

One such organization was called Aircraft-Marine Products: General information about AMP drawn from Andrew Erdman, "Staying Ahead of 800 Competitors," *Fortune*, June 1, 1992, 111–112; "AMP Incorporated History," Funding Universe.com; and "Tyco Completes Acquisition of AMP," *New York Times*, April 6, 1999.

Whitaker realized that there was need: Valerie Reitman, "Low-Key Titan Makes the Right Connections," *The Philadelphia Inquirer*, April 21, 1991 (archived at Philly.com).

And it was particularly difficult for Whitaker and AMP: Ibid.

"You can't be successful without manufacturing": As quoted in ibid.

Various reformers challenged the Church's authority: Diarmaid McCulloch, *The Reformation* (New York: Penguin Books, 2003); "Jan Hus," Wikipedia.org; "John Wycliffe," Wikipedia.org.

On the last day of October 1517: "October 31, 1517: Martin Luther Posts 95 Theses," This Day in History, History.com.

This completely unhinged Luther: McCulloch, Chapter 3, "New Heaven: New Earth: 1517–1524," op. cit.

At his trial later in the year: "October 31, 1517," op. cit.

Initially meant to disparage the dissenters: Ibid.

Americans like to drink beer: "Beer in the United States," Wikipedia.org.

Most of that beer is made by the Big Two: Elizabeth Flock, "Hopslam: How Big Beer Is Trying to Stop a Craft Beer Revolution," *U.S. News & World Report*, February 2013.

Dan Carey started working in the beer industry: Maggie Hoffman, "A Pint With: Dan Carey, Brewmaster of New Glarus Brewing Company," *SeriousEats.com*, April 8, 2010; Henry Verdon, "Ode to a Spotted Cow," *Beautiful Cupboard*, Spring 2008.

I should mention that it helps to confine your beer business: Michael B. Sauter, Alexander E. M. Hess, and Samuel Weigley, "10 States That Sell the Most Beer Are Surprising," *USA Today*, October 11, 2012.

For example, while they do market their product: "An Interview with Dan Carey of New Glarus Brewing Company," *APerfectPint.net*, August 1, 2011.

They also shrank *their distribution*: Evan Rytiewski, "The Spotted Cow Makers Remain True to Wisconsin," *Shepherd-Express*, March 14, 2013.

They urge their customers to "drink indigenous": Marcia Nelesen, "New Glarus Brewing Bottles Love for Wisconsin," *GazetteXtra.com*, July 22, 2012.

After expanding their facility in 2007: "A Pint With," op. cit.

The husband-wife team is united: Rytiewski, op. cit.

As Dan noted: Nelesen, op. cit.

As David France, director of the Oscar-nominated film: David France, interviewed by Neal Conan, "Talk of the Nation," NPR, February 12, 2013.

After a retired organic chemist, Iris Long, happened upon an ACT-UP meeting: Iris Long, interviewed by Sarah Schulman, ACT-UP Oral History Project, *ACTUPOralHistory.org*, May 16, 2003, 13.

As France notes: France interview with Conan, op. cit.

Mark Harrington, who was among those: Mark Harrington, interviewed by Sarah Schulman, ACT-UP Oral History Project, *ACTUPOralHistory.org*, March 8, 2003, 13.

Harrington credits Long with wiping away: Ibid, 15.

"We wrote to Tony Fauci": Ibid., 18.

Peter Staley, who was often the face of demonstrations: Peter Staley, interviewed by Sarah Schulman, ACT-UP Oral History Project, ACTUPOralHistory.org, December 9, 2006, 32–33.

"[W]e had this level of desperation": Ibid., 41.

Iris Long, reflecting on her involvement: Long interview, op. cit., 36.

As Peter Staley observed: Staley interview, op. cit., 41.

Chapter 8: The Elusive Art of Meaning Making

Of interest for us to the process of creating meaning: New Yorker, April 22, 2013.

"An assault weapon in the hands of a young woman defending her babies in her home becomes a defense weapon": http://www.huffingtonpost.com /2013/01/30/gayle-trotter-gun-control_n_2583098.html.

It was suggested, for example, that Mayer's policy was tinged with sexism and classism: http://www.forbes.com/sites/hbsworkingknowledge /2013/03/12/marissa-mayer-needs-to-bridge-distance-gap-with-remote -workers/.

When the ambassador from France visits Henry bearing insults and threats from the French crown prince Dauphin: Act I, Scene ii, Henry V (New York: Washington Square Press, 1960).

In Shakespeare's version, no doubt making things that much more dramatic, somehow the French have lost 10,000 troops, while the English have lost 30: "[I]t is impossible to give a precise figure for the French and English casualties. However, it is clear that though the English were outnumbered, their losses were far lower than those of the French. The French sources all give 4,000–10,000 French dead. . . . The English sources vary between about 1,500 and 11,000 for the French dead, with English dead put at no more than 100." Wikipedia, "Agincourt," April 12, 2013.

Chapter 9: How Language Creates Meaning

As Chip Souba, M.D. has written: Chip Souba, "The Language of Leadership," Academic Medicine 85, no. 10 (October 2010).

I quoted that verse of Matthew chapter 25: The Guardian, March 17, 2002.

As Belafonte recalled in a radio interview: Harry Belafonte, "News and Notes," National Public Radio, November 15, 2006.

Frost made the trip, even though he was 80 years old: Stewart Udall, "Robert Frost's Last Adventure," New York Times, June 11, 1972.

Chapter 10: Creating Meaning with Stories

One of my favorite assignments is the work we do with high-potential leaders: Harrison Monarth, personal communication.

"Do not tell stories in company": *Letters Written by the Earl of Chesterfield to his Son* (New York: Derby & Jackson, 1857).

As the storytelling expert and author of The Springboard: How Storytelling Ignites Action in Knowledge-Era Organizations, *Stephen Denning*: "Telling Tales," *Harvard Business Review*, May 2004.

When an organization's frontline employees trust their leaders: http://news .illinois.edu/news/12/1114improvementinitiatives_GopeshAnand.html.

Generations of children around the world have been raised on the classic: Watty Piper, *The Little Engine That Could* (New York: Platt & Munk, 1930).

Case in point: *A recent study from Texas Christian University had three groups of diners order from menus that listed*: http://www.nytimes.com /2013/04/30/science/exercise-versus-calories-on-menu-lists.html?_r=0.

Chapter 11: Spark the Action You Want to See

The word persuade, *on the other hand, comes in similar fashion from the Latin*: *Oxford English Dictionary*.

The journalist John Cassidy, in his interesting and provocative article: *New Yorker*, April 25, 2013.

Using frames well means both thinking well and persuading well: See the work of cognitive linguist George Lakoff.

Chapter 12: Managing Fear

As a Science Daily *report notes*: "Fear of the Dentist Is Passed on to Children by Their Parents," *ScienceDaily*, November 16, 2012.

Such fear might lead to: America Lara, Antonion Grego, and Martin Romero-Maroto, "Emotional Contagion of Dental Fear to Children: The Fathers' Mediating Role in Parental Transfer of Fear," *International Journal of Pediatric Dentistry* 22 (2012): 324–330.

The good news, if you're that parent: "Oral Health: A Window to Your Overall Health," *MayoClinic.com*, May 11, 2013.

"With regard to assistance in the dental clinic": América Lara Sacido, as quoted in "Fear of the Dentist," op. cit.

Notice what is happening to you: See, for example, Louise Altman, "Fear's Everywhere: How Are You Managing It?" *IntentionalWorkplace.com*, March 21, 2011; and Kevin Ochsner, "The Science of Managing Fears," *CNBC.com*, July 25, 2008.

The German-born spiritual teacher and author: Eckhart Tolle, *Practicing the Power of Now* (Novato, CA: New World Library, 1999), 27.

Or, you might gather additional data: See, for example, Jay M. Jackman and Myra H. Strober, "Fear of Feedback," *Harvard Business Review*, April 2003.

It isn't only the act of sharing alone that provides benefit: See John Baldoni, "Managing Your Own Fears," *Harvard Business Review Blog Network*, October 8, 2008; and Jackman and Strober, op. cit.

An article by Chloé Morrison highlights: Chloé Morrison, "In Time for Halloween, Survey Highlights Workplace Fears," *Nooga.com*, October 30, 2012. See also Liz Ryan, "Ten Signs You Work in a Fear-Based Workplace," *Bloomberg BusinessWeek/NBCNews.com*, July 13, 2010.

According to the Accountemps survey: Morrison, op. cit.

My short but substantive recommendation: Harrison Monarth and Larina Kase, *The Confident Speaker* (New York: McGraw-Hill, 2007).

Academy Award winning actor and Batman star: As cited in Serena Kappes, "5 Things You Gotta Know About Christian Bale," *People*, October 20, 2004; originally appeared in *Entertainment Weekly*.

Chapter 13: Managing Ambivalence

At one work site, union officials: Terri Peterson, personal communication.

Sandy Kristin Piderit, writing: Sandy Kristin Piderit,"Rethinking Resistance and Recognizing Ambivalence: A Multidimensional View of Attitudes Toward an Organizational Change," *Academy of Management Review* 25, no. 4 (2000): 784–786.

He was upset with the abruptness: Ibid., 788.

Piderit notes that cognitive ambivalence: Ibid., 789–791; see also Shirley S. Waing, "Why So Many People Can't Make Decisions," *Wall Street Journal*, September 27, 2010.

One such set of tools is behind the term: Richard H. Thaler and Cass R. Sunstein, *Nudge* (New York: Penguin Books, 2008, 2009).

In fact, chapter one of my last book: Harrison Monarth, *360 Degrees of Influence* (New York: McGraw-Hill, 2012), 1.

Thaler and his colleagues note: Richard H. Thaler, Cass R. Sunstein, and John P. Balz, "Choice Architecture" (essay adapted from *Nudge*), n.d., 3. http://nudges.org/tag/choice-architecture/.

Scholar Eric Johnson and his colleagues laid out: Eric J. Johnson et. al., "Beyond Nudges: Tools of a Choice Architecture," *Marketing Letters* 23 (2012): 487–504.

Johnson and his colleagues recommend: Ibid., 489.

Amos Tversky and Daniel Kahneman pioneered studies: Daniel Kahneman and Amos Tversky, "Prospect Theory: An Analysis of Decision Under Risk," *Econometrica* 47, no. 3 (March 1979): 263–292.

This is not unrelated to the status quo bias: See Daniel Kahneman, Jack L. Knetsch, and Richard H. Thaler, "Anomalies: The Endowment Effect, Loss Aversion, and Status Quo Bias," *The Journal of Economic Perspectives* 5, no. 1 (Winter 1991): 193–206; and Alana Cornforth, "Behaviour Change: Insights for Environmental Policy Making from Social Psychology and Behavioural Economics," *Policy Quarterly* 5, no. 4 (November 2009): 21–28.

Johnson and his colleagues quote learning theorist: Hobart Mowrer, as quoted in Johnson et. al., op. cit., 497.

Chapter 14: Learning from Feedback: It's Not Over 'til It's Over

He dismounted his horse and approached the troops: Frank McLynn, *Napoleon: A Biography* (London: Jonathan Cape, 1997).

In his 2005 commencement speech at Stanford, Jobs reflected on the experience: Steve Jobs, "Stanford Commencement Address" (2005), in *The Guardian*, October 9, 2011.

But eventually his perspective changed: Ibid.

"I'm pretty sure none of this would have happened if I hadn't been fired from Apple": Ibid.

When President Polk attempted to justify the war by claiming that Mexican soldiers: Roy Prentice Basler, *Abraham Lincoln: His Speeches and Writings* (Cleveland, New York: World Publishing Company, 1946).

Lincoln later regretted his attacks on Polk and the reputation it garnered him: David Herbert Donald, *Lincoln's Herndon* (New York: A.A. Knopf, 1948).

Though he proved himself a valuable and skilled soldier during the Mexican-American War: Edward G. Longacre, *General Ulysses S. Grant: The Soldier and the Man* (Cambridge, MA: First De Capo Press, 2006).

Her husband's impeachment scandal cast speculation on her as well: Jeff Gerth and Don Van Natta Jr., *Her Way: The Hopes and Ambitions of Hillary Rodham Clinton* (New York: Little, Brown and Company, 2007).

Legend has it that after his first (and last) live performance at the Grand Ole Opry, he was advised by the Opry's talent coordinator: Mark Kemp, "Elvis Presley Biography," *Rolling Stone* website, http://www.rollingstone.com/music/artists/elvis-presley/biography.

Decca Records rejected the Beatles, saying "guitar groups are on the way out": The Beatles, *The Beatles Anthology* (San Francisco: Chronicle Books, 2000).

INDEX

ABOUT THE AUTHOR

New York Times bestselling author and head of GuruMaker-School of Professional Speaking, Harrison Monarth is a leader in the field of persuasive communication, speaker coaching, message strategy and personal branding. One of the most sought-after presentation and speech coaches in the United States—he regularly prepares CEOs, senior executives, political candidates, and other leading professionals for  high-stakes presentations, leadership roles, and other opportunities to influence the agenda.

Harrison has personally coached leaders from major organizations in financial services, technology, medical, legal, hospitality, and consumer industries, as well as real estate, nonprofit, and politics. Clients include AT&T, Merrill Lynch, PepsiCo, HP, Intel, Cisco Systems, Northrop Grumman, IBM, Deutsche Post DHL, US Bank, GE, The American Heart Association, Hertz, The Ritz-Carlton, GM, and many other leading corporations, as well as political candidates and members of Congress.

Internationally, Harrison's coaching has been in demand by individuals and organizations in Berlin, Beijing, Bogota, London, Sydney, Singapore, and Tokyo, among others.

Harrison's *New York Times* bestseller, *The Confident Speaker* (McGraw-Hill 2007), is based on years of research and practice in the field of persuasive communication and high-impact speaking.

His book *Executive Presence—The Art of Commanding Respect like a CEO* (McGraw-Hill 2009) was a *Globe* and *Mail* bestseller in Canada and was named a top business book in Austria and China.

Harrison's book *360 Degrees of Influence* (McGraw-Hill 2011) was named a Top 30 business book for 2012.

Harrison is also a contributing writer at *Fortune*. He resides in New York City.